so poignantly of the cross. Pastor Parsley's
ıt of history's most important moment. It will

—JERRY FALWELL JR.
ıCELLOR AND PRESIDENT, LIBERTY UNIVERSITY

An amazingly anointed book! Pastor Rod brings the cross back front
and center and reminds us of the pivotal role it should continue to play
in the salvation of mankind. I was so touched as I read about what
a beautiful, brutal, loving sacrifice was made there by the Lamb of
God. You are bound to see the cross from a whole new perspective after
you read this!

—JAY DeMARCUS
MEMBER OF RASCAL FLATTS

I'm so delighted that my friend Pastor Rod Parsley has written a book
on the cross. Pastor Parsley has once again centered us on the most
important message in all of God's Word, and that is that Jesus died
on a cross, was buried, resurrected, and that is our hope. I hope you'll
read the book.

—GOVERNOR MIKE HUCKABEE
HOST, *HUCKABEE*

There is far too little emphasis on the importance of the cross. Jesus paid
a great price for the life and freedom we experience through that most
powerful manifestation of God's love. Without it, there is no redemption. I'm thankful that Rod Parsley has wisely sought to focus attention
on the undeniable and essential power necessary for our redemption.

—JAMES ROBISON
FOUNDER AND PRESIDENT, LIFE OUTREACH INT'L,
AND COHOST, *LIFE TODAY*

There are few voices that can be heard clearly through the postmodern
clamor that characterizes our present age. Pastor Rod Parsley sounds a
clear and constant call for a return to the discarded values of the past
in his book *The Cross*. Faint hearts will be emboldened and weak knees
will be strengthened for all those who dare to take this journey to Golgotha with him.

—DR. M. G. "PAT" ROBERTSON
FOUNDER AND CHAIRMAN, THE CHRISTIAN BROADCASTING NETWORK

Since the beginning of my professional career I have drawn strength
from the powerful preaching of Pastor Rod Parsley. In much the way I
have had success with primarily one pitch, Pastor Parsley's power comes
in a passionate, single-minded focus on the person of Jesus Christ.

That's why I'm so excited about this book on the cross—the most compelling subject matter imaginable, related by one of the church's great communicators, is absolutely a championship combination.

—MARIANO RIVERA
NEW YORK YANKEES

This could have been titled *Rediscovering the Power of the Gospel*! Every believer must read this explosive new book by Rod Parsley, especially preachers. First Corinthians 1:18—Jesus is Lord.

—KENNETH COPELAND
KENNETH COPELAND MINISTRIES

Jesus displayed His divine glory throughout His life. He preached the truth, healed the sick, raised the dead, and embodied His Father's power in the resurrection. However, no picture of His life is complete without the cross. When Jesus allowed Himself to be broken, bloodied, and lifted up on the cross, He gave us the greatest example of God's glory and love. The cross truly changed everything. Pastor Rod's powerful insights into Jesus's incredible sacrifice will forever convince you of God's passionate love for you.

—ROBERT MORRIS
FOUNDING SENIOR PASTOR, GATEWAY CHURCH

There is no gospel, no spiritual growth, and no victory without the cross of Jesus Christ. Why? These questions and more are what Rod Parsley answers as he properly reminds us that the cross is to be central to Christianity and our lives. Get your copy today!

—JENTEZEN FRANKLIN
SENIOR PASTOR, FREE CHAPEL

In his book *The Cross* Pastor Rod Parsley reaffirms our journey. You will be inspired by the truth he shares about the victory, joy, and hope we have in the cross.

—JAY SEKULOW
CHIEF COUNSEL, AMERICAN CENTER FOR LAW AND JUSTICE

There is certainly no shortage of opinions on the importance of the gospel. Those who take issue with the exclusivity of the gospel found in John 14:6 have been working overtime to downplay the true meaning of the cross of Jesus Christ. In this book, however, Rod Parsley once again reminds us all of why the cross is so vitally important to both believers and unbelievers. For it is Christ's substitutionary death upon the cross and His miraculous resurrection that provide the greatest gift ever given to mankind: salvation. Take time to read this book and be encouraged over its truths. However, let this book also be a challenge to you to share these truths with the world. For Christ and Christ alone is the only hope for mankind.

—JONATHAN FALWELL
PASTOR, THOMAS ROAD BAPTIST CHURCH

God has chosen to save the world through the cross. No route to redemption can detour around the suffering of deity. It is indispensable in the eternal plan of God. Rod Parsley in *The Cross* reveals the cross, its purpose, and its passion in language that rises to poetic heights and reaches theological depths. To Christians who—like Christ—live in a culture unready to hear His message, Parsley mounts challenges to cherish the cross, understand its power, and live out its truth."

—MARK WILLIAMS, DD
PRESIDING BISHOP/GENERAL OVERSEER, CHURCH OF GOD

Jesus's words say it all: "And I, if I be lifted up from the earth, will draw all men unto me" (John 12:32). The cross was His focus in that prophecy. Rod Parsley's *The Cross* secures that truth and the central message of all the Scriptures. It's all about redemption—and Jesus paid for it all. Now He calls us to follow His leading along the pathway of life in the light of Calvary. Thanks, Rod, for the renewal of a focus we dare not lose.

—JACK W. HAYFORD
CHANCELLOR, THE KING'S UNIVERSITY

I'm extremely happy for the new book that Pastor Parsley has written about the cross! As a follower of Christ, the cross is an essential ingredient to my faith, and it seems like we can easily overlook or forget its importance in our relationship with Jesus. In this book Pastor Parsley opens our eyes to some very important truths that we have likely neglected, challenging us to come back to our roots at the foot of the cross. Enjoy, be challenged, and transformed!

—SARAH HICKEY BOWLING
COHOST, *TODAY WITH MARILYN AND SARAH*

Pastor Rod Parsley offers a creative and compelling case for the victory of Christ and the mystery of the cross in his latest book, *The Cross*. He provides his readers with an authoritative open window into the power, glory, and magnificence of the cross of Christ with theological precision, pastoral wisdom, and rhetorical gifts from a pastor's heart and experience.

—MARCUS D. LAMB
FOUNDER AND CEO, DAYSTAR TELEVISION NETWORK

"The message of the cross is to them that perish foolishness, but unto us which are saved it is the power of God." This declaration by the apostle Paul is captured, expanded, and shared in beautiful, moving word pictures by Rod Parsley in *The Cross*. To the world the cross is a symbol of shame; to believers it is the symbol of salvation. What the world calls foolishness, we call grace. Nothing is more central to our faith than the cross, and nowhere is that message made clearer than in this book. I commend it to your prayerful reading, and I urge you to take it to heart.

—Dr. T. L. Lowery
Executive director, T. L. Lowery Global Foundation

Pastor Rod Parsley's impact as an author rivals his effectiveness as a communicator by means of television. In his book *The Cross* he sets a new standard with a comprehensive treatment of the necessity of the message of the cross of Christ to be restored in our pulpits, churches, homes, and hearts.

—Dr. Paul F. Crouch Sr.
President, Trinity Broadcasting Network

I rejoice in being able to recommend Pastor Rod Parsley's most recent book, which leads to discovering the true power of the cross of Jesus. Undoubtedly it is an essential message that the church—and the entire world—must know. Pastor Parsley is a man of God called to impact the world with the authentic message of the cross, which is Christ, who was crucified and resurrected, as well as the supernatural power and love of God.

—Guillermo Maldonado
Senior pastor, King Jesus International Ministry

The most powerful weapon in the universe is the blood of Christ and the message of the cross, which destroys Satan's most herculean weapon—death. Satan knows that if he can eliminate the cross, his plans to destroy God's plan of redemption can continue. Pastor Rod Parsley's timely revelation brings to light the significance of the cross and how Satan has weakened and warped the power of the gospel through handicapping the message of the cross. In the battle of the ages Pastor Parsley's volume brings to light the power of the cross that every believer must understand and utilize in overcoming the enemy's daily challenges of Christian living.

—Dr. Dennis Lindsay
President and CEO, Christ For The Nations

Rod Parsley's new book on the cross is a twenty-first-century classic. In this day of bloodless, powerless Christianity, this book explodes on the scene with devil-defeating power. Theologically sound and passionately written, the message of this book convicts, inspires, and calls all to a fresh commitment to the Christ of the cross. Rod Parsley has given us his best and brings the treasures of past biblical giants and their revelation on the cross. I loved it, wept and shouted all the way through it, and could not put it down. This is a must-have for every Christian. Preachers will find rich resources for preaching as well. Thank you, Pastor, for calling us to the cross…may we draw near with all our hearts.

—DR. RON PHILLIPS
SENIOR PASTOR, ABBA'S HOUSE

Reading this book, one can't help but to look to the cross and fall in love with Jesus all over again!

—DR. MEDINA PULLINGS
PASTOR, UNITED NATIONS CHURCH INTERNATIONAL

I have said for years that Pastor Parsley has been one of God's major voices, being used in a bold yet fresh way to call America and the world back to the cross. Once again it's no surprise that he rekindles our love, our passion, and our commitment to Jesus Christ by defining God's most incredible act of love—sending His Son to be the ultimate sacrifice for our sins. As you read this book, allow God to take you back to your first love.

—RON CARPENTER
SENIOR PASTOR, REDEMPTION WORLD OUTREACH CENTER

I am grateful but not surprised that God has stirred the heart and raised the voice of one of His clear apostolic and prophetic voices—Pastor Rod Parsley—in his latest book, *The Cross*, to once again challenge us to "repair the breach" through embracing the central message of our great salvation. I encourage every believer, but moreover every preacher of the gospel, regardless of denomination or ethnic persuasion, to get and read this book. I am firmly convinced that you hold in your hand a seed of "the awakening" for which we are all believing.

—CLARENCE E. MCCLENDON, PHD, DD
FOUNDER, CLARENCE E. MCCLENDON MINISTRIES

The cross slams the door on doubt. Nothing is vague. It is clear. The *only* way from earth to heaven is through the cross of Jesus Christ. Pastor Parsley's new book, *The Cross*, is a must-read for one and all.

—DWIGHT THOMPSON
DWIGHT THOMPSON MINISTRIES

In a day where the moral fabric of society is being ripped apart, God has yet again used my friend Rod Parsley as a prophetic voice of reason to call a nation back to its first love. In his new book, *The Cross*, Parsley accurately and articulately lays out the beauty and glory of the cross of Jesus in a fresh and relevant way. If you are dull in your spirit, if apathy and complacency are knocking at your door, then let this book call you back to the fiery words of Jesus, the author and finisher of our faith: "Take up your cross and follow Me." It is with great joy that I recommend this book to you!

—RICK PINO
PRESIDENT, FIRE RAIN MINISTRIES

Why did Jesus Christ die on the cross? What caused the Son of Man to do the unthinkable—to give His life as a substitute for each of us? My dear friend Rod Parsley has written a powerful book that proclaims, as the apostle Paul wrote, "I determined not to know anything among you, save Jesus Christ, and him crucified" (1 Corinthians 2:2). Through each chapter Rod reminds us that the blood of Jesus Christ is the heart of the gospel. Thank you, my precious brother Rod, for showing us once again the eternal importance of *The Cross*!

—BENNY HINN
BENNY HINN MINISTRIES

There are many discarded values that the church has lost through the years. And when we as the church lose them, it not only affects us as the body of Christ, but it also robs the lives of the people in our paths who have no knowledge of them. The cross is one of these values, but even in a time when the Pentecostal Correct have pushed the cross into our people-pleasing closets, there is a man still shouldering the responsibility that God gave each believer to share. I don't know anyone who carries the anointing to preach and teach the cross like Pastor Rod Parsley. This new book might sound like it's taking us back in time—but in reality it is taking us forward to a freedom that lasts forever. Don't live another day without this book. It is leading us back to the future where it all began—THE CROSS.

—CLINT BROWN
SENIOR PASTOR, FAITH WORLD

The tone and texture of this book is unflinchingly unapologetic, straightforward, hard-hitting, yet reassuringly optimistic and warm. The tension created between the rugged cross and the tenderness of the Christ whose love for humanity constrained Him to die for those who condemned Him to such a shameful death is riveting. The urgency of the message is compelling. The treatment of the topic is provocative. The impact of the book is convicting. Every chapter is pregnant with revelation. Intellectually ingenious, scripturally accurate, and profoundly written is how I describe this book. I could not put *The Cross* down. If there was one book that I would highly recommend, it would unequivocally be this one.

—Dr. N. Cindy Trimm
President, Trimm International

The Holy Spirit has come to this earth to testify of Jesus. The moment I started reading this book, the witness of the Spirit was so intense I could not put the book down! What an incredible masterpiece of the grace and love of God.

—Tommy Bates
Senior pastor, Community Family Church

The Cross is a must-read for every Christian. In a generation so focused on self-gratification, the message of the cross has become watered-down, outdated, and even interpreted as false. However, without this crucial piece our "Christianity" would be in vain. Many have tried to remove the cross, but no one can ever remove its power!

—Darlene Bishop
Senior pastor, Solid Rock Church

In the book *The Cross* Pastor Rod Parsley displays again why he is one of the clearest and most dynamic voices in the church today. From his roots in eastern Kentucky and central Ohio, to a worldwide platform, he sounds the clarion call to put Jesus first and to center on the cross of Christ to draw all people to salvation. This is an engaging, easy-to-read, yet hard-to-forget volume that is much needed in the twenty-first-century church. We are pleased to recommend it to you and happy to call Pastor Rod our friend!

—Dr. Steve and Kellie Swisher
Senior executives, Kenneth Copeland Ministries

THE CROSS

ROD PARSLEY

CHARISMA
HOUSE

Most CHARISMA HOUSE BOOK GROUP products are available at special quantity discounts for bulk purchase for sales promotions, premiums, fund-raising, and educational needs. For details, write Charisma House Book Group, 600 Rinehart Road, Lake Mary, Florida 32746, or telephone (407) 333-0600.

THE CROSS by Rod Parsley
Published by Charisma House
Charisma Media/Charisma House Book Group
600 Rinehart Road
Lake Mary, Florida 32746
www.charismahouse.com

Cover design by Justin Evans
Design Director: Bill Johnson

Visit the author's website at www.rodparsley.com.

Library of Congress Control Number: 2013946468
International Standard Book Number: 978-1-62136-620-1
(trade paper); 978-1-62136-621-8 (hardback)
E-book ISBN: 978-1-62136-622-5

First edition

13 14 15 16 17 — 9 8 7 6 5 4 3 2 1
Printed in the United States of America

Contents

Foreword

EVERY GOOD PARENT tries to monitor any of their teenager's habits that could lead to addiction. But since it was a Pentecostal preacher from Columbus, Ohio, whose child was addicted, what were my parents to do?

I was seventeen years old when I bought the cassette album that would become my soundtrack as a young aspiring preacher. It was called "The 25 Greatest Messages of Pastor Rod Parsley"—and from the first message I heard, I was hooked.

I lugged that big plastic binder full of tapes around with me everywhere I went. (If you're unsure what tapes are, stop reading immediately and ask your parents for an intervention.) I would make everybody I knew listen to my favorite parts, over and over again, and I would preach along with the lines I had memorized.

> We need to reach one hand into the gutter, and the other into glory, and bring the two together in a cataclysmic explosion...

Stuff like that.

My friends would ask me, "Why do you make us listen to this guy all the time?" And there were lots of reasons, really, why I loved Pastor Parsley's preaching.

- He preached with a passion that even the most aggressive punk rock bands I listened to before I became a Christian couldn't rival.

- The atmosphere in his services was so electric, the mosh pits I used to love seemed like funeral processions by comparison.

- He had a cadence and flow that, to me, sounded more soulful than Jay-Z or any other rapper on MTV at the time.

- I mean, not just anyone can pull off the phrase *cataclysmic explosion* in a sentence. You try it.

But looking back, I can see that the greatest reason his ministry moved me was because he was so completely *unashamed* of the gospel of Jesus. He lifted up—as he liked to call it—*"the blood-stained banner of the Lord Jesus Christ"* with a resolve that was sincere and searing.

That's what makes the message of Pastor Rod Parsley uniquely powerful. He is a living demonstration of the Spirit's power because of his determination to glory in the cross of Christ—without apology and without compromise.

This message of *The Cross* has never been more urgent. And Pastor Rod Parsley is the perfect man to bring the message to us, with his contagious passion, supernatural energy, and unfiltered devotion to the gospel.

You're holding a book written by a man who knows the power of the cross of Christ, both from places of deep personal pain and places of remarkable triumph and blessing.

And it's the same message he's been declaring, powerfully and faithfully, for decades.

My prayer is that God will use it to ignite the same kind of cross-fueled fire in you that He used those cassette tapes to ignite in me.

Recently I had the media team at my church transfer all those old tapes onto twenty-five CDs. Now that CD players are becoming less accessible, I'm sure I'll have them put the sermons on my iPhone soon. And when my iPhone is obsolete, you'd better believe I'll get them in another format—so I'll always have a way to play them. It won't be long before I'll be making my own kids listen to them too. I want them to hear what *real* preaching sounds like.

Why? Because the message of the cross is the hope of every generation. And Pastor Rod Parsley is a man with the boldness, wisdom, and anointing to make it real and relatable in this generation, in every situation, and in every life.

But be forewarned. Exposure to PRP may be habit-forming, highly addictive, and life altering.

—STEVEN FURTICK
FOUNDER AND LEAD PASTOR, ELEVATION CHURCH
AUTHOR, *GREATER* AND *SUN STAND STILL*

Introduction

I F MY MOST poignant and prominent memories were to form a river, its headwaters would lie in the verdant rolling hills of eastern Kentucky. Although I was born in Ohio and have lived there most of my life, my heart stubbornly calls eastern Kentucky home.

It is there, near the river that forms the border of Kentucky and West Virginia, that my parents were born and lived out their childhoods. It was there, through groves of towering sweet gums, black oaks, and roadsides bordered with honeysuckle, that we traveled to see relatives and friends more weekends than I can count. And it is there on those Appalachian plateaus that our loved ones lie in sacred repose awaiting the sound of God's gathering trumpet.

My earliest mist-shrouded memories of church, hymn singing, and Holy Spirit–conducted symphonies of prayer center around a white clapboard country church there on the edge of the Tug Fork, between Beauty and Lovely in a little town called Warfield, Kentucky. Both the town and the church were blessedly situated not far upstream from a God-constructed intersection—the confluence of two rivers. Twenty miles north of Warfield as the crow flies, the Levisa Fork and the much longer Tug Fork come together to form the Big Sandy River. It was in the hills near that intersection that my heart received the seeds of devotion that would grow and one day bloom into a lifelong love of the Savior. What an incalculable debt I owe to the men who planted those first seeds.

By the time I was two years old, my family had moved north in search of work, as so many from those parts did then, up US Highway 23 to Columbus, Ohio. We settled on the south side of the city and joined a little church on Welch Avenue. That church has since undergone two moves and a name change, but her mission remains the same—to bring the lost to a saving knowledge of Jesus Christ.

Church attendance was not optional in our house. If the doors were open, we were there together as a family. This meant Sundays, Wednesdays, and every special service and revival. Those revivals sometimes went on nightly for weeks. In other words, I logged a lot of hours in rustic church pews as a little boy.

In those impressionable formative years I recall being fascinated by the stained-glass windows that lined both sides of the Welch Avenue Free Will Baptist Church. I loved to look at them—and through them to the wider world beyond. Although each window was unique, all had one conspicuous feature in common. Each depicted a biblical scene that was superimposed on a large cross. Even though I was a fidgety boy who loved being outdoors, I enjoyed looking at those windows.

Even before I was old enough to understand a sermon or to comprehend the meaning of the songs we sang, I was already viewing life and truth through the clarifying lens of the cross.

My gaze through those windows merged with the truths that thundered from the pulpit. As the years slipped by, it seemed to me that every sermon I heard featured the cross and held it high for all to see. In fact, I can't recall hearing a single message that did not feature the cross in some way. Likewise, the hymns that resonate most vividly in my memory also had Calvary as their theme. I can still hear the congregation's voices echoing in the rafters and can still recall the words of each stanza in the heavy hymnal held in my father's strong hands. Those hymns were infused with truths about the atoning death of our Savior. One of them was Isaac Watts's "At the Cross":

> At the cross, at the cross, where I first saw the light,
> And the burden of my heart rolled away,
> It was there by faith I received my sight,
> And now I am happy all the day.

There was also "At Calvary," written by a graduate of the great Moody Bible Institute, William R. Newell:

> Mercy there was great, and grace was free;
> Pardon there was multiplied to me;
> There my burdened soul found liberty
> At Calvary.

The preaching, the music, and the architecture of my childhood all blended to leave a powerful imprint on my mind. This is why I surrendered my heart and life to the lordship of Calvary's crucified Lamb while I was still a boy. The cross was and is central to my faith—and to my life.

I am, then, honor-bound and heart-compelled not only to fill these pages with the transforming meaning of the cross of Jesus Christ but also to dedicate this book to those good and faithful servants of God who lifted up the cross to me without apology. It was under the preaching of the pioneering pastors of the Welch Avenue Free Will Baptist Church in Columbus, Ohio, that I was first introduced to the glorious cross and the ferocious love of God, which shouted from its bloodstained beam—and it is to them and those who followed them that I dedicate this book.

- 1952–1958: Reverend Delbert Gould

- 1958–1961: Reverend Fred C. Evans

- 1961–1966: Reverend Tommy Moore

- 1966–1983: Reverend Paul J. Thompson

How I revered these men. Later, in the 1960s, my family moved to the west side of Columbus, where I sat under the ministry of Reverend Clarence Newman at the West Jefferson Free Will Baptist Church. Another move a few years later took us to the southeast side of Columbus, where I was blessed by the ministry of Reverend Richard Presnell at the Williams Road Free Will Baptist Church. Another who must be mentioned is Free Will Baptist Evangelist Andrew Workman, whose preaching was instrumental in inspiring me to find and fulfill God's will for my life.

Thank you, men of God, for your fearless fidelity to a gospel with the cross at its center. Your names form an honor roll in the annals of heaven as well as in my life.

A CROSS-LESS GENERATION

Chapter 1

The mob that hounded Christ from Jerusalem to "the place of a skull" has never been dispersed, but is augmenting yet, as many of the learned men of the world and great men of the world come out from their studies and their laboratories and their palaces, and cry, "Away with this man! Away with him!"[1]
—THOMAS DEWITT TALMAGE
(1832–1902)

HEAVILY ARMED AND wearing the uniform of the Polish army, soldiers fan out across Masovian Province in eastern Poland. It is March of 1984—George Orwell's prophesied year of dictatorial mind control by the all-powerful State. It is cold, but winter is slowly losing its icy grip on communist-controlled, Soviet-dominated Poland. But on this morning a godless government endeavors to tighten its grip on the minds of a generation of Poles.

These soldiers march not to confront an invading enemy. They are headed for the district's elementary schools, middle schools and high schools with very specific orders...

"Pull down every cross from every classroom wall and door in the province."

The order has come directly from Polish Prime Minister Wojciech Jaruzelski, who, with the encouragement of his sponsors in Moscow, is in the middle of a nationwide campaign to purge Poland's public places of the vestiges of Christianity. And in a socialist-communist state, almost every place is a "public" place.

The government buildings had been first. Then came the factories and hospitals. But if the stubborn Poles are ever going to be purged of their "superstitions" and molded into good, atheistic Soviet men and women, it is vital to begin with the malleable minds of children. So, the schools are next. And the national campaign to strip Poland's children of a faith in anything other than the State is beginning in Masovian.

For as long as anyone could remember, crucifixes had guarded the walls of classrooms and lecture halls in deeply Catholic Poland. Most of the crosses removed on this day will have been hanging in place for more than sixty years—some, more than a century. And so soldiers' boots echo in the school hallways and leather-gloved hands yank countless crucifixes from countless walls and haul them to waiting garbage trucks. Yet in each violated spot on each desecrated wall something remains behind, offering silent testimony to what is missing.

On every time-weathered, soot-darkened wall is the unmistakable bright outline where a cross once hung. Yes, the government could remove the cross, but it was powerless to remove the evidence that it had once hung there.

† † † † †

Here in twenty-first-century America we've been removing our crosses too—but for the most part voluntarily. To be sure, in recent decades our highest courts' twisted understanding of "separation of church and state" has brought about the forced removal of most literal, physical crosses from the countless public squares and city seals where they had been displayed proudly and harmlessly for decades.

But what about our private places? Our homes and businesses? The cross has been disappearing here as well. We're a post-Christian culture, we're told. Furthermore, the last thing anyone in polite society would ever want to do is offend the delicate sensibilities of a skeptic or agnostic. The Taoist symbol depicting the supposed counterbalancing forces of yin and yang is ubiquitous in shops and restaurants. Chubby golden Buddhas are as well—and not just in Asian restaurants. The boldest of Christ followers may display the ichthus fish but rarely the cross. The cross seems to hold a special and singular power to offend.

But surely our churches...the houses built upon the rock of confession that Jesus is the Christ...the gathering places of those who have been redeemed by the blood shed at Calvary...surely here we'll find a bastion in which the cross of Christ is treasured and honored through both display and proclamation.

If only that were the case.

In a nation where a cross once topped every new church steeple and figured prominently in the interior architecture of every new house of worship from sea to shining sea, the cross has fallen out of fashion with architects. The cross seems so very old school, it is said. So churchy.

So…last century. For churches needing to appeal to an image-conscious public, holding the cross high is poor marketing—bad branding. Thus with accelerating frequency, modern church designers and the pastors who hire them no longer integrate the cross into their designs.

Yes, the cross is disappearing from our cityscapes and church platforms. But in a broader, profounder, and more troubling sense we've been voluntarily removing it from our hearts and minds. Silently, steadily, stealthily— without fanfare or debate—we have slipped the cross out of our preaching, from our singing, and from our daily living. As a result, the cross is fading from our collective Christian consciousness.

Yes, the cross is missing, but just as in those Polish lecture halls, a cross-shaped shadow void remains.

In a very real sense we have been midwife to a cross-less generation of born-again believers. Is that cause for concern? Indeed it is, and on the pages that follow you will see why. And before our journey is complete, you will have personally had a fresh and hopefully life-transforming encounter at the foot of the cross.

The reasons for our creeping cross-lessness are manifold. In some cases well-intentioned efforts to reach postmodern Americans for Christ have produced a cross-less version of Christianity. But as British theologian John Stott warns us in his book *The Cross of Christ*, "There is no Christianity without the cross. If the cross is not central to our religion, ours is not the religion of Christ."[2] It's true. The centrality of the cross is the hallmark of an authentic, life-giving gospel—a gospel with the power to heal not only the sin-sick, heartbroken individual but also entire cultures. Is it possible that the church's waning influence in our dark and darkening culture parallels the removal of the cross from the center of our message?

It is a culture in which many today are happy to embrace Jesus the teacher—the bringer of peaceable platitudes and lovely beatitudes about loving your enemies, turning the other cheek, and "suffering the little children." They find nothing offensive in this Jesus. Surely Gandhi had this Jesus in view when he famously said, "I like your Christ. I do not like your Christians."[3]

> The centrality of the cross is the hallmark of an authentic, life-giving gospel—a gospel with the power to heal not only the sin-sick, heartbroken individual but also entire cultures.

Even Jesus the prophet is occasionally welcome at the long table of America's growing pantheon of gods and religious icons, particularly when His prophetic pronouncements seem to call out one's preferred bad guys—whether they be the overly pious, the excessively privileged, or, for anti-Semites everywhere, "the Jews."

But more often than not the admirers of Jesus the teacher and Jesus the prophet shrink back in horror and embarrassment from Jesus the Lamb of God. This Jesus was slain for the sins of the world. Spat upon. Nailed to a tree. Writhed in His own blood. Taunted and mocked by sneering cowards who, only two days prior, would not have dared to even look Him in the eye.

The scene at Calvary is too ugly. Too shame-soaked. Its implications about sin, sin's toll, and the severe demands of cosmic justice too troubling to ponder for long. "No, you can keep your shattered Jesus of the cross," the spirit of the age seems to say. "If we must have a Jesus, and we'd prefer not to, we'll take the pretty Sunday school illustration version with children on His lap."

And thus a generation silently slips the cross down from its conspicuous hook on the wall of its theology. Pleasanter, less demanding images are found to hang in its place.

Today in some churches, if the cross is mentioned at all, it is often only to warp its meaning and message into something more palatable to the modern sensibility. Thus, a stream of new books call for "reimagining" or "reinterpreting" or "rethinking" the cross of Christ.

Back in the middle part of the last century the influential pastor of the Riverside Church in New York City, the late Harry Emerson Fosdick, famously said that the traditional view of the cross and the doctrine of the atonement made Christianity a "slaughterhouse religion."[4] He also suggested the idea that Jesus suffered as a substitutionary sacrifice in our steads because of our sins was a "pre-civilized barbarity."[5]

Building on that argument, some prominent leaders in the Emergent church movement today—many of whom are admirers of Fosdick and were deeply influenced by his teaching—seek to re-brand the astonishing events at Golgotha. They would have us think of it as a wonderful example of self-sacrifice and servanthood that we should all strive to emulate (in less blood-soaked ways, of course) rather than as a judicially necessary sacrifice of an innocent—payment for the sin-guilt of the entire human race.

Indeed, one of the most prominent of those leaders, Brian McLaren, author of the book *A New Kind of Christianity* (an apt title because it is impossible to square McLaren's views with the old kind), has argued forcefully and widely for a view of Jesus's sacrifice as something other than a once-and-for-all payment for mankind's sin. He says, "The view of the cross that I was given growing up, in a sense, has a God who needs blood in order to be appeased. If this God doesn't see blood, God can't forgive."[6]

In a 2006 interview McLaren expanded upon this theme by sympathetically summarizing the views of a friend:

> And I heard one well-known Christian leader, who, I won't mention his name, just to protect his reputation, because some people would use this against him. But I heard him say it like this: The traditional understanding says that God asks of us something that God is incapable of Himself. God asks us to forgive people. But God is incapable of forgiving. God can't forgive unless He punishes somebody in place of the person He was going to forgive. God doesn't say things to you—Forgive your wife, and then go kick the dog to vent your anger. God asks you to actually forgive. And there's a certain sense that, a common understanding of the atonement presents a God who is incapable of forgiving. Unless He kicks somebody else.[7]

If there has ever been a more heartbreakingly warped characterization of the sacrificial act of a loving Father-God and willing Redeemer-Son, this preacher has never heard it. The following comes close, however.

In his book *Reimagining Christianity* (there's that word!), Episcopal priest Alan Jones repeats this idea that God never intended Jesus's sacrifice on the cross to be considered a payment for our sins: "The Church's fixation on the death of Jesus as the universal saving act must end, and the place of the cross must be reimagined in Christian faith. Why? Because of the cult of suffering and the vindictive God behind it."[8]

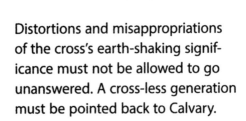

Distortions and misappropriations of the cross's earth-shaking significance must not be allowed to go unanswered. A cross-less generation must be pointed back to Calvary.

It should come as no surprise that many of these teachers speak and write admiringly of Gandhi. They seemingly share his view of the cross. "I could accept Jesus as a martyr, an embodiment of sacrifice, and a divine teacher," Gandhi wrote in his autobiography. "But not as the most perfect man ever born. His death on the cross was a great example to the world, but that there was anything like a mysterious or miraculous virtue in [the cross], my heart cannot accept."[9]

In the chapters to come we will explore these questions and assertions in the unfailing light of Scripture—indeed in the illuminating radiance of the cross itself. For these distortions and misappropriations of the cross's earth-shaking significance must not be allowed to go unanswered. A cross-less generation must be pointed back to Calvary.

Of course, the New Age campaign to reshape the cross into an image less contrary to humanistic sensibilities is not a new one. More than one hundred years ago the great evangelist Charles Spurgeon glimpsed the emerging trends around him and said:

> But I will tell you what Satan's favorite scheme is nowadays; it is not to oppose the cross, but to surround the cross, and try to get the cross to alter its shape a little. Men who hate the doctrines of the cross, say, "We, too, preach the gospel." They alter it; they misshape it; they make it "another gospel, which is no gospel at all."
>
> Let others say, if they will, that yes and no can meet together; that fire and water can kiss each other; that Christ and Belial can be twins: the true minister of Jesus Christ cannot do that. Truth is truth; and whatever is the opposite of it cannot be truth. That which opposes truth must certainly be error and falsehood. But it is the fashion nowadays to try to blend the two things together.[10]

If it was the "fashion" among preachers and teachers back in Spurgeon's day, what word should we use to describe the current campaign of revisionism and distortion?

God's sworn enemy has always despised the teaching of the cross above all other messages, for Golgotha was the scene of Satan's complete and final defeat. That is why any preacher inclined to focus on other topics will have plenty of subtle encouragement from the bitter, vanquished deceiver who lost everything on that hill.

Dr. Martyn Lloyd-Jones was a powerful Welsh preacher who was born early enough (1899) to be moistened by some of last falling raindrops of the great Welsh Revival. As a very young man early in his ministry, Lloyd-Jones preached one night at a church in South Wales. Following the service, an older deacon at the church who had been an eyewitness and participant in that historic move of God pulled the young preacher aside and gently offered an observation. "Reverend Lloyd-Jones, I have heard you speak on several occasions now. It seems to me the cross of Christ has little place in your preaching."

Years later Lloyd-Jones would recall that he was stung by the older man's rebuke. In response he found and bought two books about the work of Christ on the cross. He spent a full day and a night in his study reading and re-reading them, neglecting both food and bed. The next morning he emerged and announced to his wife that he had discovered "the real heart of the gospel and the key to the inner meaning of the Christian life."[11]

Dr. Lloyd-Jones spent the next sixty years preaching the cross and the blood shed upon it throughout Great Britain and beyond—influencing an entire generation of British preachers. Late in life, silver-haired and raspy-voiced, he was still thundering the same message with which he had emerged from that study all those years earlier:

> There it is then. It is in the whole of the Scriptures. What right have you or anybody else, what right has any ecclesiastic, to get up and pour his scorn upon the blood of Christ, and to say the cross does not

matter, that it is the teaching we want, or that it is the imitation of the person that we need? The whole of the New Testament is proclaiming the blood of Christ, the death of Christ upon the cross, on Calvary. It is the heart and centre of the Christian evangel, the good news of salvation.[12]

> It is at the foot of the cross, and there alone, that we can look with horrified wonder upon the raw ferocity of God's love for a fallen race.

Today the temptation to adopt a mode of preaching in which the "cross of Christ has little place" is more powerful than ever. In contrast, the apostle Paul declared, "But God forbid that I should glory, save in the cross of our Lord Jesus Christ, by whom the world is crucified unto me, and I unto the world" (Galatians 6:14). Paul did not shrink from the cross. Nor did he seek to "reimagine" it so as to refit it to his own preferred worldview. He "gloried" in it.

Of course he did. The cross is the hinge-point of human history. It is the fulcrum of God's grand, brilliant lever—four thousand years in the crafting—that in a single day pried a fallen world from Satan's soul-killing grasp. It is at the foot of the cross, and there alone, that we can look with horrified wonder upon the raw ferocity of God's love for a fallen race.

To accept it and glory in it—this is the only truly rational response.

There is awful beauty in the blood shed on that

skull-shaped hill. But many can't see it. They have not been taught how. The nineteenth-century evangelical Anglican bishop J. C. Ryle said:

> I declare I know no greater proof of Man's depravity than the fact that thousands of so-called Christians see nothing lovely in the cross. Well may our hearts be called stony, well may the eyes of our mind be called blind, well may our whole nature be called diseased, well may we all be called dead, when the cross of Christ is heard of, and yet neglected. Christ was crucified for sinners, and yet many Christians live as if He was never crucified at all![13]

There is an unspeakable loveliness to be seen at the cross—if only we have eyes to see it.

We have created a cross-less generation. Yet, paradoxically, crosses are seemingly everywhere. They dangle from chains around the necks of whole constellations of godless gyrating pop stars. Elite professional athletes adorn their bodies with crosses, displaying tattoos that sometimes span the entire breadth of a torso. Some of these ink-stained warriors indeed know the Jesus of the cross they display. Many do not—but have simply appropriated the sacred symbol as just one more hip affectation.

At the same time, if a cross makes an appearance in a town square or school program, it triggers a fainting spell and three lawsuits. Indeed, in 2012 the folks at the Freedom From Religion Foundation conducted a multipronged campaign of cross removal across America that would make Poland's Jaruzelski proud. These efforts included a pressure campaign focused on getting the city of Woonsocket, Rhode Island, to remove from a local fire station a white cross-shaped memorial to local soldiers killed in World War I.[14] That monument—clearly inspired by the famous World War I–era poem "In Flanders Fields"—has stood harmlessly and nobly in place for more than ninety-one years. "In Flanders fields the poppies grow / Between the crosses, row on row..."

Meanwhile, a man submerges a crucifix in urine, snaps a Polaroid, and declares it "art." He is celebrated for his "courage."

How is it possible our culture has found a way to both trivialize and marginalize the most significant emblem to ever emerge from the rushing river of history? How can we simultaneously banish the cross and profane it? How is it possible that the First Amendment can at once be construed to protect the public display of so-called art that defiles a cross but not to protect a schoolteacher's wearing of a cross-shaped lapel pin? How, in fact, can it be argued that this same First Amendment actually strips the teacher of that right?

Any society that successfully manages to hold such wildly dissonant, utterly irreconcilable views at once has slipped into a very special form of madness.

Madness...but there is a cure. Like judgment, application of this remedy must first begin at the house of God. The church can't possibly hope to speak to a lost and hopeless world unless she first returns the cross to its rightful place in her heart and in her message. That place is in the center.

"But what about the resurrection?" some may protest. "Shouldn't that be our primary focus?" Without a doubt, the importance of Christ's resurrection to our faith and our message cannot be overstated. But without the cross there could have been no resurrection. There can be no joy of Easter Sunday without the sorrow of Good Friday. Indeed, the resurrection displayed God's power. But at the cross it is God's love on display before the astonished eyes of both earth and heaven.

This book you now hold in your hands aspires to a lofty aim: to help you, the reader, recalibrate your thinking about the Christian faith and put the cross of Christ at the center where it belongs. This is your invitation to embark on an amazing but difficult journey—a journey to Calvary's hill.

Some of the sights will be awe-inspiring. This epic expedition will take you into the heights of the spiritual realm where you'll glimpse what most human eyes could not perceive on the day Jesus offered up His life—the cosmic, behind-the-scenes battle that took place in the heavenlies for the souls all mankind. You'll also see some things that are hard to look upon—as you confront the grim reality of what Roman crucifixion truly entailed. In exchange for the horror, you'll gain a life-transforming understanding of the price paid to make you whole and His.

The chosen path will take us deep into the mysterious territories of what the Bible calls "the foolishness of the cross" and the "scandal" of Jesus's sacrifice. Along the way you will come to understand that in His atoning suffering and death Jesus purchased much more for you than merely a ticket to heaven. Indeed you'll discover seven glorious "exchanges"—the knowledge of which will leave you unwilling to live another day beneath your privileges as a son or daughter of God.

We will silently join mother Mary and beloved John at

the foot of the cross and simply listen in awe. We will hear the seven last "words" of Christ and mine each precious syllable for meaning, insight, and encouragement.

Finally, we will find ourselves at home once more—with a monumental choice to make. We'll explore what Jesus means when He asks, "Take up your cross and follow Me."

You've been warned. Portions of the journey will not be easy. But what power, provision, and peace await those who make this pilgrimage to the summit of Calvary.

But what of those confiscated crosses in Poland all those years ago? Was that the end of it? Was the operation to surgically remove the cross and all it represents from the minds and hearts of a nation's children a success? In the spirit of the late radio broadcasting legend, Paul Harvey, it is important you know "the rest of the story."

One of the schools that was purged of its crosses on that late winter's morning in 1984 was in the little town of Garwolin. There soldiers entered the main school and removed seven large crucifixes that had hung on the walls of its lecture halls since the 1920s.

It is important to understand that the cobblestone streets of Garwolin were no strangers to oppression, tyranny, and the echo of soldiers' boots. In the seventeenth century more than 90 percent of the town's population had died in a massive invasion from Sweden that came to be known by the surviving remnant simply as "The Deluge." And three hundred years later, when Hitler's blitzkrieg bombers darkened the skies over Poland followed by Panzer divisions of tanks and Nazi storm troopers, more than 70 percent of the city's structures had been leveled.

No, the people of Garwolin knew well what it meant to have the will of outsiders imposed upon them by force of might and arms. But they also knew the power of raw, stubborn resistance. So as dawn broke on the following morning, students arrived to find new crosses occupying the spots where the old ones had been. Under cover of darkness the parents of the students had entered the building and replaced them with their own hands, using crosses from their homes.

So the drama replayed itself later that day. Soldiers entered. Crosses were torn down. Bare walls testified silently of their violation with bright cross-shaped outlines.

The next day two-thirds of the school's six hundred students showed up at the school to protest the action. Most of these were carrying crosses, although some of these were little more than two pieces of wood hastily wired together into a crude "T" shape. But they were crosses, nonetheless. Then heavily armed riot police arrived.

The throng of cross-bearing children was driven into the streets by the police, so the children raised their handmade crosses heavenward and marched to the refuge of a nearby church. To their surprise, they soon found themselves joined by more than twenty-five hundred other students from nearby schools. Together they began praying and singing hymns about the crucified Savior.

Soon soldiers encircled the sanctuary, but not before the international press had arrived. Almost instantly images of a throng of singing students holding crosses high above their heads were appearing on television screens and newspaper pages all over the planet.

Within five years of this day, Poland would have its first free and fair elections since falling behind the iron curtain at the end of World War II. A year after that, Lech Wałęsa, father of the Solidarity Movement, would rise to the presidency—ending Poland's long, dark night of totalitarianism.

Of course, the Solidarity movement was already a gathering force for change before the events of this day. Indeed, the fuse of this gentle revolution had been ignited in 1979, when a Polish Catholic by the name of Karol Wojtyła made a nine-day pilgrimage back to his native Poland under his new title, Pope John Paul II.

More than a third of the nation's population turned out to hear the Polish pope in his various stops throughout the nation. And as he preached a history-shaking sermon before one million Poles assembled in Warsaw's Victory Square on June 2, the throng responded with a fourteen-minute ovation of applause that spontaneously morphed into congregational singing. With one voice they sang *"Christus vincit, Christus regnat, Christus imperat* [Christ conquers; Christ reigns; Christ governs]."

Five years later, the showdown over the crosses of Garwolin served to focus an uncomfortable spotlight on the very point at which the Soviet Empire's weakening wall of Marxist inevitability seemed to be crumbling most rapidly.

There is no triumphant, culture-transforming Christianity without the cross.

On that day, television cameras brought a watching world the words of a courageous local priest who addressed the weeping crowd in the church. They heard him say, "There is no Poland without a cross."

One thing is certain. There is no triumphant, culture-transforming Christianity without the cross.

We stand at an intersection—a literal *cross*roads of history—in which for many, even those with a genuine love for God and His Word, the cross has lost its centrality. Quietly, imperceptibly, hands have removed the cross from its rightful place in our thinking, in our praying, in our loving, and in our serving. And yet...where it once hung, there remains an unmistakable, bright outline marking the spot.

Yes, the modern theologians and the forces of secularization have done their best to remove the cross, but they cannot erase the evidence that it once hung there—just as in those Polish lecture halls a cross-shaped shadow void remains. This is, in a sense, a blessing. Because the void tells us precisely where it needs to go. Come along as we rediscover the power, majesty, and beauty of the cross. Let us learn anew how to appropriate that power to our lives.

Here begins a journey to restore what has been stolen from us. And as is so often the way with journeys, this one begins at an intersection.

AT THE INTERSECTION OF HEAVEN AND EARTH

Chapter 2

The cross is the centre of the world's history;
the incarnation of Christ and the crucifixion
of our Lord are the pivot round which
all the events of the ages revolve.[1]
—ALEXANDER MACLAREN
(1826–1910)

S OME SAY IT lies in the city center of Bangalore, India. Others believe that to find it, you must travel to downtown Shenzen—southern China's bustling financial center. But many are convinced that the title of Busiest Traffic Intersection on this blue marble planet belongs to the spot where Avenue Ipiranga crosses Avenue Rio Branco in downtown São Paulo, Brazil. Gridlock in that spot once spawned a legendary traffic jam more than 165 miles long.

Still, others say it is human bodies that should be counted when awarding this prize, and therefore we should look to Tokyo's Hachiko Square—a rectangular space that sees more than a million pairs of feet each day and with as many as ten thousand people crossing during a single "walk" cycle of the light.[2] (And I thought waiting on the ten kids in front of me in the hot dog line on Saturday night at Mrs. Bailey's was "busy.")

Those who study the science of urban traffic flow, however, believe they have found their champion in Dhaka City, the capital of Bangladesh and home to 11 million inhabitants. There you will find a spot where South Road crosses Zahir Raihan Road, with Dhaka City's busy bus depot nestled in the arms of these traffic-clogged streets.

At any given moment of any given day, the intersection is filled with buses approaching or departing the depot. The spaces in between the buses are filled by thousands of cars and taxis. Any and all remaining space between these is in turn filled by innumerable motorcycles, motorized rickshaws (called *tuk-tuks*), and bicycles. Now imagine all of these drivers utterly ignoring the designated lane lines and freely disregarding the traffic signals. It is an astonishing sight. This indeed may be the busiest intersection on earth, but the debate continues.

What is not in dispute is the site of the loneliest intersection in history—the place that no one desired to come to and yet, the very place where all humanity must be summoned to make their appearance.

It is the intersection of two rough-hewn beams of wood. One stands vertical—pointing simultaneously to heaven and hell. The other is horizontal and serves to mark an invisible line, parallel to the surface of the earth and extending outward to circle the planet. It is this planet that fell victim to a curse when its designated steward-lord willfully forfeited control to an outlaw deceiver.

This cosmic crossroads sits atop a skull-shaped hill near the garbage dump, outside the walls of the capital of a troubled backwater province on the periphery of the vast

Roman Empire. Look now. At the center of this wooden intersection hangs a solitary figure—the prince of heaven, abandoned in a prison of loneliness with only silence and suffering for cellmates.

His closest friends have fled in fear and shame. In fact, in a craven act of naked self-preservation one of His two closest friends has denied he even knows Him. The throngs that have followed Him, hung on His every word, partaken freely of His healing power, joyously received their dead back from the grave at His command, eaten miraculous meals of fish and loaves wrought by His hands—these have all scurried home and bolted the door, save the handful who now stay behind to hurl taunts and insults at Him.

At this intersection hangs a man so utterly alone that even the omnipresent Father God Himself hides His face and withdraws his comforting essence. *"Eloi, Eloi, lama sabachthani?"* cries the man on the cross in Aramaic. "My Lord and my God, why hast thou forsaken me?" (Mark 15:34).

In the twenty centuries since that anguished cry rang out across the barren Judean hills, countless people have speculated as to why Jesus would utter it. He seems to express surprise and bewilderment—two things Jesus never once showed in His previous thirty-three years on earth.

The fact is, Jesus was not expressing surprise. He was quoting Scripture. Specifically, He recites Psalm 22:1—a "messianic" passage that not only expresses the psalmist David's heartache in the moment but also looked prophetically forward through the centuries to the day his descendant, the promised Messiah, would deliver and redeem the whole world through His suffering.

The lonely figure hanging in the intersection is a Man of Scripture. Indeed, an astonishing percentage of the red-lettered words in our Bibles are direct references to Old Testament passages. Jesus of Nazareth has defined His life, His mission, and His message purely and wholly in terms of God's Word. It seems that every circumstance and every challenge brought a scripture to Jesus's lips. When confronted by the devil, Jesus quoted Scripture. He cited it to answer His disciple's endless questions. He quoted it to refute and confound the Sadducees, Pharisees, and Sanhedrin. And now... alone, to whom will the author of our salvation quote such immortal words? No one remains to hearken to His eternal utterances.

As the accumulated sin and depravity—every sickness and disease, every satanic spell and demonic depravity— of an entire race fall upon one Man, a pure and holy Father is forced to withdraw His life-giving, comforting presence from His only begotten Son. As Jesus feels His Father pull away—as He learns for the first time in His eternal existence what it means to be separated from God the Father—a scripture comes to mind. Only one.

Jesus knows that in dark moments we must cling to the eternal truth and everlasting triumph of God's Word. And in the darkest and most desperate moment any person has ever been called upon by divine demand to endure, His tortured and tormented soul reaches out, grasping for anchoring comfort. So He quotes this messianic prophecy to remind Himself of who He is, what He is doing, and why it must be done. He reminds Himself why He must *not* do what you or I or any other mortal in His place and with His power would do. He must not call forth a legion of angels to come rescue Him while striking every arrogant, depraved mocker dead in his tracks. No, the work He has begun must be finished.

Never has a person been so alone, so abandoned, as was Jesus of Nazareth on the day He felt the hateful bite of that angry cross. The mighty revivalist of a former era, G. Campbell Morgan, explained it. He said:

> It is impossible to follow the Lord into the place of His mightiest work. Alone He entered and wrought. No man followed Him, nor could follow Him at all, in help, or in sympathy, or in understanding. Fallen man was degraded in will, emotion, and intelligence, and therefore was not able to help, or sympathize, or understand. From that inner mystery, therefore, man was excluded.[3]

The witnesses to the crucifixion of Jesus the Christ perceive some remarkable things on this day. Human eyes see three men being executed in the manner reserved for the very worst of Rome's enemies and criminals. They see the earth cloaked in a darkness even midnight would not recognize. Ears hear the loathsome whistle and snap of the scourge, the ring of hammer on spike, horrifying shrieks of agony, and the demon-fueled laughter of angry soldiers. Witnesses feel their stomachs turn, and they stumble without balance. The earth shakes and quivers beneath their feet as an earthquake rumbles through the Judean hills. And in the air, the acrid scent of burning flesh wafts down into the valley from the temple above where a thousand Levitical priests make haste to sacrificially offer tens of thousands of spotless Passover lambs before the sun's last ray of light is extinguished and the day is done.

It is an almost overwhelming scene to completely comprehend. Even so, infinitely more is taking place beyond the reach of the five human senses. In the invisible realm of the spirit the battle of the ages is reaching its climax. Here—at the loneliest moment since God Himself allowed the first tick of time to expire—a drama is unfolding if only we'll have eyes to see it. As Jesus hangs bolted on that brutal beam at the intersection of heaven and earth, we must look behind the silver veil of the natural realm to glimpse the full reality and revelation of the cross of Christ in three critical aspects.

First, Calvary's cross is the place where God's unfathomable provision intersects with our deepest and most basic need. Put another way, it is where the furious love of God Almighty encounters our broken and shattered hearts.

Never before or since has such love been on open display as it was on Calvary's tree. Words fail. The intellect staggers. As the late Richard John Neuhaus wrote in *Death on a Friday Afternoon*: "All the theories of atonement are but probings into mystery, the mystery of a love that did not have to be but was, and is."[4] Spurgeon put it this way, "Come, Believer, and contemplate this sublime truth, thus proclaimed to thee in simple monosyllables: 'He laid down His life for us.'"[5]

Calvary's cross is the place where God's unfathomable provision intersects with our deepest and most basic need.

"Does Jesus really love us?" you ask. My wife's, Joni, favorite author, Brennan Manning, said it as powerfully as it has ever been proclaimed when he said:

> The compassion of Jesus, He is the compassion of Almighty God, and Jesus says to your heart and mind, "Don't ever be so foolish as to measure My compassion for you in terms of your compassion for one another. Don't ever be so silly as to compare your thin, pallid, wavering, depending on smooth circumstances human compassion with Mine, for I am God, as well as man." When you read in the Gospels that Jesus was moved with compassion, it is saying His gut was wrenched, His heart torn open, the most vulnerable part of His being laid bare. The ground of all beings shook, the source of all life trembled, the heart of all love burst open, and the unfathomable depths of the relentless tenderness was laid there. Your Christian life and mine don't make any sense unless in the depth of our beings we believe that Jesus not only knows what hurts us, but knowing, seeks us out, whatever our poverty, whatever our pain. His plea to His people is, "Come now, wounded, frightened, angry, lonely, empty, and I'll

meet you where you live. And I'll love you as you are, not as you should be…because you're never gonna be as you should be." Do you really believe this? With all the wrong turns you made in your past, the mistakes, the moments of selfishness, dishonesty, and degraded love? Do you really believe that Jesus Christ loves you? Not the person next to you, not the church, not the world. But that He loves you—beyond worthiness and unworthiness, beyond fidelity and infidelity. That He loves you in the morning sun and in the evening rain. Without caution, regret, boundary, limit. No matter what's gone down, He can't stop loving you. This is the Jesus of the Gospels.[6]

Certainly the living Christ demonstrated beyond degree His voracious love for us. He proved it to us in His *incarnation*—willingly forsaking the privileges and glory of heaven to trudge through the mud, muck, and mire of this cursed planet. He laid aside His glory and eternal majesty like a cloak and leaped into an earthly manger amid the lowing of the horned oxen, the bleating of the sheep, and the scent of the straw. He lay down in a barn because that is, after all, where a lamb should be born.

In His incarnation he said, "I will prove to you that I am your friend because I will become as you are." Not deity humanized. Nor humanity deified. All God, and yet all man.

He also proved His love by His *association*. The religious crowd despised Him for His habit of dining with all the "wrong" people. He refused to keep His distance. He openly allowed adulteresses to wash His feet. He freely accepted dinner invitations from tax gatherers. He laid His heavenly hands upon unclean lepers. He awakened each morning and waded out neck deep into the unwashed, indecent, polluted, diseased, corrupt, broken, frightened, and hurting hordes of humanity.

He did not shrink back in horror at our repulsive evil or our abhorrent and malignant wickedness. He ran to us and threw His arms around us. He came to the disenfranchised. He sought out the discontented. He embraced the disconnected fringes of society. This is how He "*so*" loved us!

He proved to us that His love for us was without limitation or boundary and impossible to measure when He prayed for us. The seventeenth chapter of John offers us an extraordinary opportunity to slip silently, breathtakingly close to Jesus and eavesdrop as He pours out His heart interceding for us. He prays that we'll experience joy. He prays with specificity for our protection. He prays that we'll become the beneficiaries of the power and blessing that become available through unity with the Father and with each other. And later, in that garden where the war with self-will was waged and where the capillaries of His face burst at the thought that He might fall short at accomplishing His Father's will by dying there, having never made it to the cross, and He bled through the skin of His face, He proved it when He spoke our vile names upon His sanctified lips. He, emboldened by love, without embarrassment, called us brothers and sisters. He made our hope His purpose.

His love was palpable and tangible in His prophecy and preaching. His every proclamation brought light and life. But perhaps the sermon that best described His mission and motive was His simple three-point message about a lost coin, a lost sheep, and a lost son.

A woman (we are not told her name) has lost her coin. She has spent the daylight hours searching the cracks and corners of her humble home. She has wearied herself sweeping the floor over and over again. The rugs and carpets have been moved and now lie rolled up outside on the lawn. The furniture is stacked up on one side of the room. That coin is of great value and simply must be found. Now the light is failing. She can no longer carry on the search upright. So she begins to lower herself and crawl upon her hands and knees—probing every crevice of her floor and walls.

Jesus's story is an allegory. You understand that there was no woman. There was no lost coin. You do realize, don't you, that He is speaking of Himself? And of you?

Leap forward in time a few weeks from the preaching of this masterful message and see the blessed Jesus crawling on His bleeding hands and knees, a heavy wooden crossbeam biting into His back. Can you see the King of glory on His hands and on His knees, searching every crack and crevice of Calvary's rugged hillside? He is looking for somebody.

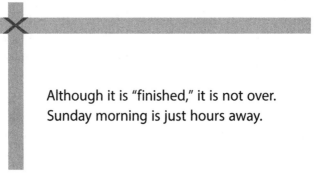

Although it is "finished," it is not over.
Sunday morning is just hours away.

What if we dared bend down to tap Him on the shoulder in this monumental moment and ask, "Master, how is it possible that You should be in this position?" His reply to us would be, in a quivering yet determined tone, "I've lost one. I have to find her. For I came to seek and to save that which is lost."

Yes, Jesus proved His friendship in His willingness to become one of us, in His willingness to be with us, and in His proclamation that He was sent on a mission of purpose to reclaim us…but most of all that love and friendship were proven once and for all—beyond all question—on that cross. Can you see Him? There He hangs, pale and pallid, bleeding from every pore of His body, bloodletting by which the very veins of God Himself were emptied. And with every red drop that flows from His riven side and runs freely down His naked flank and drips off His toes into bloody pools on the earth…each splash says, "I'm doing this for you." Truer words have never been penned than these, "What a friend we have in Jesus."

Here at this lonely intersection He suffers in anguish, agony, and distress. Here He dies. Here He declares, "It is finished." But although it is "finished," it is not over. Sunday morning is just hours away.

Second, Calvary's cross is the place where God's ultimate triumph intersects with Lucifer's consummate demise. In fact, Jesus's death and resurrection represent God's victorious "checkmate" of Satan in a cosmic chess match that had been thousands of years in the playing. It was a match made requisite by humanity's rebellious, pride-fueled fall from dominion stewardship over the earth.

There in that garden in the middle of paradise, our pristine parents had been fiendishly deceived into surrendering their God-granted authority and their keys to the kingdom. The terrible and tragic result was mankind's severing loss of intimate connectedness to God. One exposure to Satan's corruption carried the communicable condition of sin and contaminated the bloodstream of Adam's entire race. The entire earth was now subjected to degeneration, decay, and death. The contemptible and cruel curse had commenced.

God's opening gambit in the chess match of the ages was to prophetically declare to His serpentine opponent that one day a descendant of the first woman, her "seed," would arise to put a victorious foot upon the usurper's head—even as the serpent would be permitted to but "bruise his heel" (Genesis 3:15).

The next several thousand years of human history, and the entirety of the Old Testament record, can best be understood as the unfolding of God's strategic intent to bring that "seed" into the earth—and the serpent's futile efforts to keep that very scenario from ever becoming a redemptive reality.

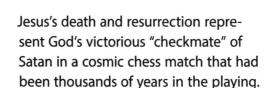

Jesus's death and resurrection represent God's victorious "checkmate" of Satan in a cosmic chess match that had been thousands of years in the playing.

Move and countermove, the match unfolded.

- Cain's murder of Abel; the birth of righteous Seth

- Abraham's cowardly surrender of his lovely wife Sarah to a foreign monarch's harem; a dream that warns that monarch before he takes her into his bedchamber

- Pharaoh's slaughter of an entire generation of Hebrew infants; the miraculous rescue of the infant Moses by an Egyptian princess

- King Saul's repeated attempts to murder David; David's survival and rise to the throne of Israel

- Herod's "slaughter of the innocents" in Bethlehem; the preemptive dream that warned Joseph to whisk his wife and infant son away to the refuge of Egypt

Each of these events and countless others leading to the crossroads of Calvary are highly calibrated moves in this consuming chess match. And the "spoils of war" are the souls of all mankind and the title deed to planet Earth. This is the significance of the "scarlet thread of redemption" that runs and rambles like a crimson red river through the Bible's wondrous narrative—from its origin "In the beginning" to the finality of its repose "It is finished." Every move, every strategy imposed displays a loving, redemptive, brilliant plan to plant that promised "seed" in the fertile soil of earth and the doomed flailing serpent's desperate, fear-and-rage-filled efforts to keep that seed from coming forth in manifested glory.

In the light of this understanding, look with fresh eyes as John the Revelator attempts to communicate the magnificent truth divinely displayed to him, describing this cosmic contest:

> And there appeared a great wonder in heaven; a woman clothed with the sun, and the moon under her feet, and upon her head a crown of twelve stars: And she being with child cried, travailing in birth, and pained to be delivered. And there appeared another wonder in heaven; and behold a great red dragon, having seven heads and ten horns, and seven crowns upon his heads. And his tail drew the third part of the stars of heaven, and did cast them to the earth: and the dragon stood before the woman which was ready to be delivered, for to devour her child as soon as it was born. And she brought forth a man child, who was to rule all nations with a rod of iron: and her child was caught up unto God, and to his throne.
>
> —REVELATION 12:1–5

That dragon, the serpent of old, had no prospect of preventing the birth of that prophesied promised Seed, so he sought to eliminate Him as soon as he broke the womb of his mother. He attempted to destroy the Seed by having every boy under the age of two in an entire province murdered. When that failed, he tried corrupting the Promised One when He was at His weakest and most vulnerable—at the end of a forty-day fast. That too failed. When the Seed came to maturity as a man and spoke unfiltered, unvarnished truth, the dragon filled religious hearts with such rage that they sought to throw Him from a cliff.

Finally, after months of scheming and manipulation...when the serpent had successfully filled the hearts of the religious establishment with envy and jealous rage...when he had even gained twisted influence over the mind of a member of Jesus's own inner circle...Satan finally became intoxicated on his own lie and allowed himself to believe that he could triumph. He thought that he had been successful in having God's own Son arrested, tried, beaten, scourged, and nailed to a cross as a criminal—completely unaware that his actions were fulfilling the masterful plan of the Almighty. By the time the sun had set on that holy and historic Passover Friday, the pure and broken heart of the Prince of God had stopped beating.

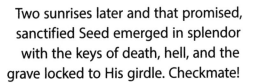

Two sunrises later and that promised, sanctified Seed emerged in splendor with the keys of death, hell, and the grave locked to His girdle. Checkmate!

"Check!" thought a smug and jubilant devil. "This match is finally over, and I have won," he hissed as demon hordes clapped their fettered hands together. "That Seed, promised to that...woman...all those millennia ago has failed. I've done my worst to the best that heaven had to offer, and now that pathetic Prophet's mouth is silent; that Seed's eyes are now blind; that Commander of wind and wave, that Healer of the suffering sons of men is now lying lifeless, still, and cold in a guarded, borrowed tomb just over the hill there. And as a result of my conquest, men will never again feel the warmth of love or walk in the light of grace—they will forever know God as a liar, and sin will rule and reign in their depraved hearts forever!"

We now know that Satan, that ancient Grand Master deceiver, had fallen into his own trap. As evil Haman hung on the gallows he built for righteous Mordecai, so Satan devised his own demise. This was the wisdom of God on display, for... "Had [the princes of this world] known it, they would *not* have crucified the Lord of glory" (1 Corinthians 2:8, emphasis added). The site of what the enemy of our souls believed to be his greatest victory was, in actuality, the scene of his absolute annihilation. He had miserably failed to comprehend in his blighted, over-inflated opinion of his own power and pride what Jesus had told His disciples on a hillside outside Jerusalem on His way to the Feast of Passover one afternoon: "Verily, verily, I say unto you, Except a corn of wheat fall into the ground and die, it abideth alone: but if it die, it bringeth forth much fruit" (John 12:24).

Two sunrises later an angel shouted. Two sunrises later the earth shook. Two sunrises later the stone was rolled away. Two sunrises later and that promised, sanctified Seed emerged in splendor with the keys of death, hell, and the grave locked to His girdle.

Checkmate!

Third, and finally, the cross of Calvary's crucified Lamb is where the bankrupt culture of a fallen race encounters the transformative power of sacrificial servanthood. In other words, Golgotha is not the singular site of Satan's defeat. It is more than just the place where you and I find adoption and restoration—as deeply amazing as that is. It is at this intersection that whole nations and entire people groups can be made perfectly whole. The leaves of Calvary's tree are for the healing of the nations.

William E. Sangster, a fiery Methodist preacher in the early part of the last century, told the story of taking a young boy from the rural English countryside into one of Britain's grand Gothic cathedrals for the very first time.

> The cross of Calvary's crucified Lamb is where the bankrupt culture of a fallen race encounters the transformative power of sacrificial servanthood.

Once the pair's eyes grew accustomed to the dim lighting, the boy looked up above the altar and gasped, "There is a cross up there!" The old preacher paused, thought for a moment, and then pointed to the floor of the cathedral. "There's a cross down here too," he said. The boy looked down at the floor in confusion for a bit, looked around at the massive room studying each detail, then eventually a broad smile dawned across his face.

"The *cathedral* is a cross," he said in wonder. It was true. With the long center aisle of the nave flanked by alcoves on either side of the altar, the footprint of the hulking structure formed the shape of a perfect cross.

Whenever he told this story in a sermon, Sangster would follow it by saying, "You can take me to the foot of Golgotha and say, 'There is a cross up there.' And you would be correct. But I will point you to the earth and say, 'There is a cross down here.' The cross is in all of life. It is in the earth. It is life's foundation."[7]

The crucifixion of Jesus Christ occurred at a very specific point in God's timeline of history in a very specific spot on planet Earth. Most believers can tell you that the events of Good Friday occurred around AD 33 in the ancient city of Jerusalem. But what most Christians do not understand is that the cross and its implications transcend time and place. Please remember that when the apostle John was granted a glimpse into the heavenly realm there on the isle of Patmos, he witnessed Jesus being introduced to heaven's adoring host as "the Lamb slain before the foundation of the world" (Revelation 13:8).

Herein is a mystery few understand. Within it lies the key to transforming a culture bent on self-destruction via self-absorption. We must understand that the principles displayed at the cross were woven into the very fabric of the universe from the beginning by the hand of the Creator. In other words, "there's a cross down here."

We've already heard Jesus articulate one of those principles when He said, "Unless a grain of wheat falls into the ground and dies, it remains alone" (John 12:24, NKJV). He pointed the way again when He said, "Greater love hath no man than this, that a man lay down his life for his friends" (John 15:13). Over and over Jesus proclaimed and modeled the principle of the cross to His disciples.

"If you want to lead, you must serve," He told them. But they could not understand, so in His final hours the Crown Prince of heaven stripped to the waist and washed their filthy feet as if He were the lowest slave in the household. "Give, and it will be given to you: good measure, pressed down, shaken together, and running over will be put into your bosom," He cried (Luke 6:38, NKJV). But that made no sense to them, so He said, "Hide and watch," gave away His very life, and then inherited a seat at the right hand of God.

There is a cross down here. Love your neighbor. Do good to those who despise you. These principles make no sense in the context of postmodern, rationalistic, materialistic America. They are the antitheses of Darwinian self-preservation. They cut against everything the earthly princes of Wall Street and Hollywood Boulevard and Pennsylvania Avenue hold up as truth.

> The principles displayed at the cross were woven into the very fabric of the universe from the beginning by the hand of the Creator.

There is a cross down here. But the church has forgotten meekness and humility in an age of ostentatious pride and self-aggrandizement. We've lost sight of the truth shouted from the top of Calvary's mountaintop by a battered, bleeding man with a sign reading "King" nailed above His head...that service and self-sacrifice, and most of all love, are our keys to influence and victory.

Yes, there is a cross up there. Thanks be to a loving God who did not withhold His precious Son but freely gave Him up for us. But there is a cross down here too. Jesus hung at the intersection of heaven and earth. And in a sense, so do we.

WHY A CROSS?

Chapter 3

Jesus was not crucified in a cathedral between
two candles, but on a cross between two thieves;
on a town garbage heap; at a crossroad of
politics so cosmopolitan that they had to write
his title in Hebrew and Latin and in Greek; at
the kind of place where cynics talked smut and
thieves cursed, and the soldiers gamble.[1]

—GEORGE MACLEOD
(1895–1991)

I N THE AUTUMN of 1968 a Jerusalem archeologist
named Hershel Shanks received a phone call that
would change his life. It seems a construction crew had
been doing some earthmoving for a new housing project
just north of the Old City, in an area known back then
as French Hill. One of the bulldozers had unearthed what
appeared to be some ancient burial chambers, the excited
voice on the other end of the line explained. Shanks, an
employee of the Israel Department of Antiquities and
Museums, was being dispatched to investigate.

What the young archeologist found when he arrived at
the site were a series of tombs that would later prove to be

part of a huge Jewish cemetery complex dating from the period of the second temple.

The first tomb Shanks investigated was a cave-like opening carved out of the soft, white limestone that is ubiquitous in the Jerusalem hills. It consisted of two chambers, each with a burial niche carved into the wall. What awaited him in one of those chambers proved to be one of the most significant finds in the history of biblical archeology.

On entering he found an ossuary, a stone burial box, containing the bones of a deceased person. On the side of the box a name had been scratched. It read: "Jehohanan (J pronounced Y) son of Hagakol." Jehohanan was between twenty-four and twenty-eight years of age.

This was a common form of burial in the first century. The family members would initially entomb the body of a deceased loved one, then wait a year or so for the body to fully decompose. Then they would return, carefully disassemble the skeletal remains, and place them in the ossuary for permanent storage in the tomb. Such bone-filled ossuaries are uncovered in Israel all the time. But something about one of the bones belonging to the man named Jehohanan was different. In particular, the heel bone of the man's right foot rocked the academic worlds of both history and archeology. You see, that heel bone had an iron spike more than four and a half inches long sticking though it. Sideways.

Jehohanan had been crucified.[2]

The discovery sent shockwaves through the world of archeology because, as surprising as it may seem, no archeological evidence for the practice of crucifixion had ever been found prior to this day in 1968. Even so, no serious scholar doubted that the Romans and other cultures had made wide use of the practice for hundreds of years. There was far too much contemporaneous written evidence testifying of the grisly practice.

For example, Roman governmental records concerning a slave revolt led by Spartacus in 71 BC describe how the Roman army lined the road from Capua to Rome with six thousand crucified rebels.[3] That's one cross every 88 feet for 104 miles. After King Herod's death in AD 7 triggered a minor Jewish uprising, the Roman legate Quintilius crucified two thousand Jews in Jerusalem.[4] And as the armies of the Roman general Titus surrounded Jerusalem in 70 just as Jesus had predicted (Luke 21:20), Roman troops crucified roughly five hundred Judeans a day for several months.[5]

It wasn't just the existence of a spike running through the heel bone of a man who had lived and died approximately the same time as Jesus of Nazareth that made it such a groundbreaking discovery. No, it was the *way* the nail impaled the bone that really set the biblical archeologists on their ears—suggesting that almost every painting or depiction of the crucified Jesus ever rendered is wrong in a key aspect. The spike had pierced the man's heel bone from the side—not the foot from the front. We'll explore that aspect shortly. But in the light of these facts, a number of questions leap to mind.

First of all, if crucifixion was so commonplace and deployed on such a large scale, why was Jehohanan the first body to ever be discovered showing the clear signs of having suffered in this way? And what purpose did crucifixion serve for the Romans?

The troubling questions as to how and why the Romans

employed this method of execution leads us to more relevant questions. Namely:

- How did the Lamb of God and Savior of all mankind make the ultimate sacrifice? Just how did Jesus die?

- What, as best we can know, did He experience?

- And why did He have to experience it? Could not the Son of God have died in some other way and still have fulfilled His role and satisfied divine justice?

- Does it matter *how* the Savior of the world dies?

Yes, the Bible makes it clear that the principles upon which a just and holy God founded our universe demanded that a sinless representative of mankind had to die. But there are many ways to die.

Why a cross?

This is not pleasant ground we're about to cover here. But I promised you a journey up Calvary's hill to stand at the foot of the cross. What we will see there will be hard to look upon, but we will be forever changed for having seen. Better. Stronger. More grateful. More yielded. More fit for the Master's use. That is why this cross-less generation of believers must return to the foot of Calvary.

When I survey the wondrous cross
On which the Prince of glory died,
My richest gain I count but loss,
And pour contempt on all my pride.

See, from His head, His hands, His feet,
Sorrow and love flow mingled down!
Did e'er such love and sorrow meet,
Or thorns compose so rich a crown?[6]

Yes, we need to look. We must look. But to truly take in that scene requires some understanding of the nature and context of the Roman practice of execution by crucifixion. The whys and hows are as illuminating as they are disturbing.

> What we see at Calvary's cross is hard to look upon, but we will be forever changed for having seen. That is why this cross-less generation of believers must return to the foot of Calvary.

For the Romans, crucifixion actually began not as a form of execution but as a form of punishment. It was designed as a form of torture—one used on a specific type of individual with a specific purpose in mind. That specific type? Slaves. The purpose? To terrify the rest of the enslaved populace into compliant servitude.

Shortly before the time of Jesus's birth in Bethlehem, under the reign of Caesar Augustus, the Romans adopted crucifixion as an official punishment, but only for slaves and foreigners who rebelled against Rome's authority, never for Roman citizens. Individuals with official Roman citizenship enjoyed certain civil rights that other subjects of the Caesars did not. You may recall the passage in Acts 22 in which the apostle Paul is about to be scourged by a Roman centurion. He is tied up and stretched out at a whipping post, but just before the lictor's lash was released to peel his flesh from his bare back, he mentions that he is a Roman citizen. That news had a dramatic effect:

> The chief captain commanded him to be brought into the castle, and bade that he should be examined by scourging; that he might know wherefore they cried so against him. And as they bound him with thongs, Paul said unto the centurion that stood by, Is it lawful for you to scourge a man that is a Roman, and uncondemned?
>
> When the centurion heard that, he went and told the chief captain, saying, Take heed what thou doest: for this man is a Roman. Then the chief captain came, and said unto him, Tell me, art thou a Roman? He said, Yea. And the chief captain answered, With a great sum obtained I this freedom. And Paul said, But I was free born.
>
> Then straightway they departed from him which should have examined him: and the chief captain also was afraid, after he knew that he was a Roman, and because he had bound him.
>
> —ACTS 22:24–29

The same was true for crucifixion. In fact, only slaves convicted of certain crimes were punished by crucifixion. In crucifixion's earliest forms, a rebellious slave would have a heavy wooden beam placed horizontally on the back of his neck and his arms stretched out and tied to it with cords. The slave would be forced to parade up and down the streets of the city announcing his offense. This was designed to inflict both pain and humiliation while serving as a warning to other slaves.

The highly public shame and degradation were key components of this type of punishment. But because the main purpose of this practice in its early form was to punish, humiliate, and frighten disobedient slaves, it was usually not fatal.

Of course, someone eventually surmised that if a little bit of pain and humiliation did some good, then perhaps more of each would do even more good. Thus the practice of crucifixion devolved—taking on ever-crueler manifestations. Eventually, beating or scourging was added to the process. Later, the forced marching through the street was consummated with the attaching of the cross beam to an upright post—usually at a busy intersection. Often the upright portion of the cross (*a crux simplex*) was set in a permanent place and used over again many times, since wood was extremely precious in Palestine at the time.

Shock and awe was the preferred method of keeping subjugated peoples in line. And few things delivered more shock value than seeing a would-be leader of the people beaten half to death and nailed to a high pole.

Only in later times, probably in the first century BC, did crucifixion change from being a cruel punishment to one of the cruelest forms of execution ever devised.

As we've already noted, if the goal is to kill a criminal, there are much more efficient ways to do so. But killing a criminal wasn't the sole, or even the primary, purpose of crucifixion. It was designed to horrify and intimidate a population into docile subjection.

By the time Jesus, the Son of God, stepped into the timeline of human history, Rome was an occupying power all over the known world. And by then the Romans had long since learned that the key to maintaining the famed *Pax Romana* was ruthlessly crushing rebellion the instant it began to be evidenced. Shock and awe was the preferred method of keeping subjugated peoples in line. And few things delivered more shock value than seeing a would-be leader of the people beaten half to death and nailed to a high pole. The spectacle served as a sort of grotesque billboard for the irresistible might of the Roman state.

In the twenty centuries since the Romans crucified a certain itinerant prophet-preacher from Nazareth, there has been much disagreement and speculation about the precise details of how He was slain. The reason for this is that the Romans displayed great creativity, flexibility, and ingenuity in the various methods and means they employed to carry out these executions. In times of war or rebellion, when it became necessary to crucify hundreds and even thousands of individuals in a short period of time, necessity became the mother of invention. But in peacetime the Romans had the luxury of spending time imagining how they could magnify and apply every morose detail of suffering methodically and meticulously.

The same technological prowess that covered the world in Roman roads...the same engineering genius that produced astonishing viaducts and aqueducts that still function to this day...was brought to bear on the task of making examples of and eliminating perceived threats to the all-powerful state.

Thus crucifixions were carried out in accordance with certain rules, using only those who were specially trained physically, mentally, and emotionally for their somewhat demented profession. Under "normal" circumstances crucifixions were only carried out at designated locations. In Jerusalem, the capital of the Roman province of Judaea, that place was just outside the city wall and near one of the gates—a place called Golgotha.

Let us now, from a short distance, follow Jesus through the lonely, grueling, final hours of His pre-resurrection life. One by one we'll see His closest friends and followers shrink away and cower in fear. We'll need to summon our greatest courage if we're to make it with Him all the way to the summit of that hill called, literally, *the skullcap.*

Under the cold, ghostly light of a full Passover moon, Jesus leads His inner circle to the familiar sanctuary of the Mount of Olives. A garden there, Gethsemane they call it, has been a frequent refuge for prayer. Here He is usually His most relaxed and at ease. But tonight as they approach, the Master becomes more and more agitated— more troubled than His disciples have ever seen Him, with the possible exception of that recent day in which He'd single-handedly cleared the temple courtyard of racists, con artists, and hucksters. That was clearly righteous anger at work. But tonight…this is different. This looks more like…dread.

He begs His disciples to pray with Him, but they are too distracted. Too overwhelmed by their personal concerns about their private agendas. Too weary. Too worn. They seek and quickly find the numbing solace of sleep. And so He wrestles all of hell all night, all alone.

On His knees He wages a mighty battle with a legion of whispering, taunting demons and with His own very human will. Of course, He is well aware that unthinkable, unspeakable physical pain awaits Him in the hours to come. But it is not the prospect of such agony of soul and physical pain that attempts to fill His heart with fear. The man who once went forty days without food in the desert has already faced and conquered physical pain. He knows the crushing avalanche of shame that is about to fall down upon Him…but it's not the tsunami of filth and defilement roaring toward Him that fills His heart with despair. He knows the sin, the guilt, and the shame of every person who has ever lived or ever will live is about to be poured into His pure soul—the guilt of every pedophile, every rapist, every selfish user, every cruel abuser, the prideful, the arrogant, the murderous, the sadistic, the twisted—and you and me at our worst. The One who has never known the slightest taint of sin is about to become sin on our behalf.[7] Our Canaan King does not fear any of this, but rather our Royal Troubadour is terrified and in such agony and anguish at the thought that He may die here—in a garden—where the first Adam died. He convulses at the reality that if He is overcome and succumbs to death's icy grip here, He will never fulfill His prophetic destiny, and the Father's plan and purpose will never be realized. This garden represented Satan's last opportunity to destroy the seed first announced in Genesis 3, and from the day God gave that promise of propitiation in verse 15, Lucifer had only one objective: Jesus must die anywhere *but* on that cross! To do so would leave the human race depraved and forever separated from the source of all life. No, He could not die here; He must not die here. He must survive this so He can die on that ugly, that hateful, that mean and cruel cross so that redemption would become the song available to Adam's entire race. In that garden He prays, and that prayer is understood by its interpretation by the writer of Hebrews: "Who in the days of his flesh, when he had offered up prayers and supplications with strong crying and tears unto him that was able to save him from death, and was heard in that he feared" (Hebrews 5:7).

So He prays. Let us draw a little closer and listen. What will be the first word from His anguished lips?

"Abba!"

> Gethsemane was ground zero in the supreme battle of the ages. As it was with Jesus, so it is with those who follow Him—the greatest satanic resistance always comes just before your breakthrough.

He cries out, as if in pain and panic, using the term that is the first spoken word of every infant in every Aramaic-speaking land. "Abba! If it be Thy will, let this cup pass from Me, but nevertheless, whatsoever Thou wilt." In response to this prayer, we see an angel come—dispatched directly from the throne room of His anguished Father—strengthening the Son lest He be completely overwhelmed by the demonic assault. Nevertheless, the battle is far from over.

Gethsemane was ground zero in the supreme battle of the ages. As it was with Jesus, so it is with those who follow Him—the greatest satanic resistance always comes just before your breakthrough.

> And being in an agony he prayed more earnestly: and his sweat was as it were great drops of blood falling down to the ground.
>
> —LUKE 22:44

The medical specialists tell us of a rare condition called *hematidrosis*. It occurs when the capillary blood vessels that nourish the sweat glands rupture, allowing blood to freely intermingle with sweat. The afflicted individual literally sweats drops of blood. This condition is usually brought on by extreme mental anguish or life-threatening stress. And indeed, in this moment Jesus confesses to His heavenly Father, "My soul is deeply grieved, to the point of death" (Matthew 26:38, NAS). Here, in modern terminology, He is saying, "I am scared to death." He was not frightened to die; He was born to die—just not here. He told His disciples just that, and when Peter disagreed, He rebuked him, calling him a devil.[8]

The cross was His only objective, for the cross was the only destination that would satisfy divine justice. After a second season of solitary prayer, it is clear that Jesus has, as the old Pentecostal intercessors used to say, "prayed through." This first crisis is over. Though He is physically exhausted, He is strengthened in soul and spirit. So He rouses His drowsy friends in time for them, and us, to see Him arrested by an armed mob dispatched by the corrupt and privileged defenders of the religious status quo.

They take Him to the house of the high priest, and here Jesus will endure the first of several increasingly severe beatings He will receive over the next few hours. He will also feel the sting of hearing Peter's vehement denial of association. The complete and utter desertion of the very One who is a "friend who sticketh closer than a brother" has begun in earnest.

> The cross was His only objective, for the cross was the only destination that would satisfy divine justice.

Now we must follow the jeering, cursing throng to Pilate's doorstep. Roman law decreed that outside of Italy, only a Roman procurator held the power to impose death by crucifixion. This is precisely why the Gospels record Jesus being passed from Pontius Pilate, the procurator of the province of Judaea; to Herod Antipas, the regional ruler of Jesus's home territory of Galilee; and back again.

Making this round-trip requires a walk of roughly two and a half miles through a gauntlet of unimaginable abuse. Jesus has not slept. His face is bruised and swollen from the beatings. The hematidrosis has most likely left His skin painfully tender.

As Roman law dictates, once a defendant is found guilty and is condemned to be crucified, the process must be overseen by a crucifixion specialist known as the *Carnifix Serarum* (literally, the "flesh nailer").

In strict accordance with Roman law, Pilate orders Jesus to be flogged as a precursor to the actual crucifixion. As we stand watching, in stupefied horror, inconspicuously amid the crowd of gawkers, the Son of God—the One who spoke with such power and poetry about the way God clothes the lilies of the field with beauty—is stripped naked. He is forced to face a massive stone column and leather straps are attached to His wrists, allowing soldiers to stretch His beloved arms, which were strong enough to stop the tempestuous sea and gentle enough to hold the little children, around the curve of the column, thereby stretching the skin of His back taut.

The cursed whip consists of several strips of leather with a series of stone beads or metal balls spaced periodically along the length of each strand. At the tip of each strip is a jagged fragment of sheep bone hewn and filed sharp as a razor. The wielder of the whip is an expert in his ghastly craft—trained to inflict maximum pain and damage but without killing his victim. The "criminal" must be alive and conscious when hung upon the cross. Only then can the crucifixion have its desired effect upon the onlookers. As the flogging commences, not only are the back and sides of the One who healed blind men with His touch involved, but also the buttocks and legs are given due attention as well. Some of our fellow onlookers who have witnessed many such floggings begin to murmur. There is something different about this one, they say. The man wielding the whip is normally detached...almost bored. But on this day an unseen force seems to animate him, filling him with rage and a vindictive joy. Some begin to wonder aloud if there will be anything left alive for the Flesh Nailer to work with.

Finally, and suddenly, it is over. The volume of blood now pooled around the base of the column is astonishing. His piercing eyes are now swollen shut from repeated blows from dozens of fists, beard partially yanked out at the roots, and the devastating effects of the flogging have rendered Jesus of Nazareth essentially unrecognizable. Even so, the worst is yet to come.

We see one of the soldiers handed something by an onlooker in the crowd. It is a purple robe and a crown of thorns, both intended to mock the idea that this direct descendant of King David, through His mother, Mary, might be the rightful wielder of the scepter of Judah.

The woven ring of thorns is jammed brutally down upon His hemorrhaging brow, and the robe is thrown over the raw and torn flesh of His blood-soaked back. We witness another demon-inspired round of spitting, punching, and taunting before the robe is ripped from His back, reopening His wounds, and is replaced by a rough-hewn wooden crossbeam that, in His deplorable and depleted condition, He must now carry.

The mercilessly long walk in the sweltering heat up through the narrow cobblestone streets of ancient Jerusalem, through the Sheep Gate, and up to the crest of the skullcap hill begins as insects bite, flies swarm and buzz, and dogs howl from the scent of fresh blood. The Lamb is being led to slaughter. But Jesus—due to massive blood loss, injury, and dehydration—is going into shock. Halfway there He crumbles under weight of the crossbeam, and though demanded to do so, He cannot rise. A black face from the crowd appears; a man named Simon from the North African coastal city of Cyrene rushes to aid the fallen King. Although the black race has borne many a heavy burden, there have been none to match the load Simon carried on the darkest day of deeds in devilish infamy.

At the head of this process we now see a soldier carrying a wooden placard with some words written upon it. This too is prescribed by Roman law. The sign is called the *titulus*, and the writing on it states the criminal's name and his crime. Later this sign will be nailed above the crucified man's head. We catch a glimpse of the *titulus* and for the first time can read what is written there. In three languages we see:

Jesus of Nazareth. This is the King of the Jews.

After what seems an eternity, we arrive at the pinnacle of the designated place of crucifixion. From our vantage point just outside the Sheep Gate we can look directly across the valley and see the massive "veil" of woven fabric that covers the entrance to the temple. Today, the eve of Passover, the temple courtyard is a hive of activity. The crucifixions of two other men—a pair of common thieves—are already underway. Their screams are echoing through the Tyropoeon Valley.

We witness in anguish as Jesus is hurled to the ground and roughly stretched out upon the crossbeam that had been delivered and deposited by Simon. A five-inch-long spike is struck by a hammer, driving it crashing through sinews and flesh. As His nerves contort in horrible spasms, with great precision both nails find their marks in each wrist just below the base of the hand and sink deeply into the wooden beam. Then, with aid of ropes and pulleys, the beam, with the man attached, is hoisted up and into place atop the vertical post. The force of the beam dropping into place immediately jerks both arms out of their shoulder sockets. Jesus, our Savior, dangles there momentarily, but the Flesh Nailer has two more spikes in his hand.

He takes hold of one of Jesus's feet and positions it, not at the front of the vertical beam but at the side. Then he drives the spike sideways, through the thickest portion of the ankle bone, and on into the post. He repeats this with the other foot on the other side of the post. This aspect of the process of crucifixion would be lost to history for almost two thousand years. For twenty centuries paintings and statues would depict Christ crucified with his feet, overlapping, in front of the post, secured by a single nail. Only the discovery of an ankle bone belonging to one of Jesus's contemporaries, who too had been crucified, would correct this misconception.

Jehohanan, son of Hagakol, was a young Jewish man who may have come from a wealthy and intellectual family, since one of his family members was identified as participating in Herod's lavish building of the temple. Jehohanan's bones' revealed clues indicated that even though he had a cleft palate, he was a well-formed and handsome man and that he never had to do any hard physical labor. But despite his advantages, it appears that Jehohanan was condemned for political crimes or possibly even seditious activities again the Roman government. When he was crucified, the nail being driven sideways through his right heel bone struck a knot inside the olive wood post into which it was being driven. This knot was so hard the iron spike curled and bent under the force of the hammer. As a result, when it came time for Jehohanan's grieving family to remove his body from the cross for burial, they could not remove the spike without further maiming his lifeless body. So they interred him with the spike still piercing the bone. And two millennia later it would be there, shards of olive wood still clinging to the metal.

One of the horrors of crucifixion that both Jehohanan and Jesus would have experienced is the inability to breathe normally while hanging in that distorted position. Hanging from the arms in such a way actually makes it impossible to exhale. To do so requires pushing upward out of that horrible sag of death, bearing all of the victim's body weight on his nail-pierced feet in order to relax the muscles of the chest wall enough to permit exhalation. But obviously doing so was excruciating. Indeed, our English word *excruciating* is actually derived from the same root as crucifixion.

The Romans learned early on that men would die within hours, and sometimes minutes, from asphyxiation as they became too weak from shock to push themselves upward. And the Romans weren't interested in providing any quick deaths—prolonged and protracted suffering on display was their aim. The psychological impact of a crucifixion on a community was much more powerful and lasting if the victim survived for quite some time.

In order to prolong the anguish and therefore enhance the propaganda value, Roman executioners added a feature to their crosses that would keep the tormented victim alive for extended periods of time—sometimes for days on end. It was the *sedile* (some say "sedulum"), a small shelf or seat attached to the front of the cross, about halfway down. This device provided some support for the victim's body and may explain the phrase used by the Romans, "to sit on the cross."

In other provinces throughout the empire, the Romans leave their crucified criminals undisturbed to die slowly of physical exhaustion, shock, or blood loss. But they have had to alter this grisly practice here in Judaea. Jewish tradition requires burial on the day of execution. Therefore, in Palestine the executioner will break the legs of the crucified person in order to hasten death and permit burial before nightfall. Indeed, the leg bones found in the ossuary of Jehohanan were both broken, and the right one shattered.

> The Romans weren't interested in providing any quick deaths—prolonged and protracted suffering on display was their aim. The psychological impact of a crucifixion on a community was much more powerful and lasting if the victim survived for quite some time.

In keeping with this practice, we watch as a Roman soldier goes to each of the two thieves on either side of Jesus carrying something akin to a sledge hammer. With powerful, practiced blows, he fractures both legs of each of the condemned men. Now rendered incapable of pushing themselves upward to breathe, they will die of asphyxiation within minutes.

Now with malicious intent, the same solider approaches the suffering Christ impaled upon the middle cross. He prepares to swing the hammer but then notices that Jesus's chest no longer rises and falls in a desperate struggle to breathe. A quick jab of a spear into the side as one would poke at a slain animal in the field confirms the obvious. He is already dead.

But only moments earlier, just as Jesus, gasping and wheezing, whispered a few final words, and as His mother, Mary, who watched with wonder when He inhaled His first breath, in woe witnessed Him exhale His last, one of the soldiers in attendance noticed something odd happening across the valley inside the temple complex. There was frantic commotion and shouting throughout the courtyard. At first he thought he'd had too much wine because it looked to him as if that massive fabric doorway tapestry hanging at the entrance to the temple had split down the middle. What he did not understand was that a door had been left ajar by God Himself offering that long-anticipated invitation—let all who will, come.

Debates continue in the theological world about the type of cross used when Jesus was crucified. There were four that were commonly used by the Romans. The most convenient would have been a tree, living or dead, with the trunk and branches providing the means by which the victim could be nailed or tied. But since trees did not always grow in sufficient numbers or appropriate places, other means were devised. Some crosses were no more than a post, pole, or stake set in the ground, with the victim's hands and feet nailed to it.

Other versions of the cross became known as the high tau or low tau, taking their names from their resemblance to the Greek letter *tau*, or *t*. The high tau had its crosspiece on the top of the vertical post, while the low tau was assembled with the horizontal beam farther down. The vertical beam was fixed in one location while the cross-beam was carried by the victim to the crucifixion site as part of their public humiliation.

From what we know from the record of the Scriptures, as well as contemporary history and archeological discoveries, it is likely that Jesus died on a low tau cross, which became known as the Latin cross and has become a universally recognized symbol of Christianity.

Did it really matter how the promised Savior died? Why a cross?

After all, Jesus was accused by the religious establishment of heresy. And heretics were customarily stoned. In fact, the fledgling church's very first martyr, Stephen, was stoned by an enraged mob for speaking what they believed were heresies—even as a man from Tarsus named Saul looked on approvingly. Why wasn't Jesus simply stoned?

Jesus, the "Lamb of God who takes away the sin of the world" (John 1:29, NKJV), was the living fulfillment of every type and shadow embodied by the Passover lamb. The tens of thousands of Passover lambs being sacrificed over on the Temple Mount the day Jesus was crucified died by the knife of a Levitical priest. Had Jesus similarly been run through with a Roman sword, would His shed blood have been just as efficacious?

As Neuhaus suggested, our explorations of the cross are only "probings into mystery."[9] But the Bible gives us clues and insights into this—the greatest and most terrible of all mysteries.

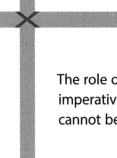

> The role of Jesus's shed blood is imperative and must not be, indeed cannot be, overemphasized.

First, the Word of God makes it clear that the shedding of the Messiah's innocent blood was a vital aspect of His sacrifice. And the Roman process of crucifixion was an appallingly bloody affair. As the writer of Hebrews emphatically declares, "Without shedding of blood is no remission" of sin (Hebrews 9:22). On the eve of His death, Jesus Himself pointed symbolically to a cup of wine and said, "For this is my blood of the new testament, which is shed for many for the remission of sins" (Matthew 26:28).

Therefore, if biblical accuracy and authenticity are our aspiration, the role of Jesus's shed blood is imperative and must not be, indeed cannot be, overemphasized. However, the mission of Jesus... the reason He left heaven's splendor and became the Second Adam... was to roll back the curse that descended upon the entire human family, including the earth, which they inhabited when the first Adam fell from grace into dis-grace.

That infamous act of upright rebellion took place at a tree—the tree of the knowledge of good and evil. And for reasons we may not fully understand this side of glory, there is something significant about a death on another tree that points back to that fall and its resultant curse. In Deuteronomy 21:22–23 (emphasis added) we find:

> And if a man have committed a sin worthy of death, and he be to be put to death, and thou hang him on a tree: his body shall not remain all night upon the tree, but thou shalt in any wise bury him that day; (*for he that is hanged is accursed of God;*)…

The Hebrews of Jesus's day were very attuned to the implications of this passage. They viewed crucifixion as the worst fate that could befall any Jew. Such a person was under a curse and irredeemable. But it was the apostle Paul who, by divine inspiration and revelation, grasped the full curse-repealing implications of death on a tree. He had those implications in mind when he penned Galatians 3:13: "Christ hath redeemed us from the curse of the law, being made a curse for us: for it is written, Cursed is every one that hangeth on a tree."

Yes, the shedding of that spotless blood—a blood utterly untainted by the stain of sin—was absolutely essential to effect a redemption that could pass legal muster in the court of heaven. But a sacrificial death that would once and for all time annihilate the curse spawned by rebellion had to be an obedient death on a tree. There had to be thorns at that tree because thorns were a God-declared outcome of that curse's unfolding.[10] It had to be a naked and shameful death because the very first indicator that Adam and Eve had fallen under the potent power of sin was their shame-filled realization of their own nakedness.

There was no other possible death for that "Seed" promised to Eve. The One whose heel the serpent would bruise (and oh, how His precious heel was bruised!). The One who, in His victory over death, would crush the head of that serpent of old and make all things new.

It had to be a cross.

LISTENING AT THE CROSS

Chapter 4

*Seven words! The sacred seven-number of Scripture,
denoting completeness. It is the full gospel of
salvation from the lips of the dying Saviour. Verily,
O Jesus, "grace is poured into Thy lips," and to
all eternity we shall "wonder at the gracious
words which proceeded out of Thy mouth," when
hanging as a curse for us on the tree of Calvary![1]*
—ROBERT H. IRELAND
(1928–2012)

FINAL WORDS ARE important. We have always been
fascinated by the last words uttered before one's life
on earth expires. Could this be because we contemplate in the deep recesses of our soul what it feels like to
face death? Do we wonder what goes through the mind
when a person knows he or she is about step over into
whatever awaits in the life to come?

On his deathbed the immensely powerful and wealthy
movie studio kingpin Louis B. Mayer is reported to have
whispered, "Nothing matters...nothing matters," in the
final moments before he slipped off into eternity. When
movie legend Joan Crawford breathed her final words

on this planet, the story goes that only her housekeeper was present to hear them. Crawford was in the midst of a heart attack when her longtime employee walked into her room. The maid, a Christian, instantly began to pray for her employer. Crawford heard the intercession, swore, and snapped, "Don't you dare ask God to help me." According to the story, those were the last words she'd ever speak.

Gravely ill, the anti-Christian French philosopher Voltaire begged his doctor for a miracle the physician was powerless to deliver. "I am abandoned by God and man," Voltaire said to his practitioner. "I will give you half of what I am worth if you will give me six months' life." When the doctor could give him no hope, Voltaire bitterly replied, "Then I will go to hell and you will go with me."[2]

As these stories testify, the passing of the godless and the ungodly is often less than graceful. Not surprisingly, the saints of God tend to utter words of a markedly different character.

For example, the final words of Prince Albert, husband of Queen Victoria, were, "I have had wealth, rank, and power, but, if these were all I had, how wretched I should be. Rock of Ages, cleft for me, let me hide myself in Thee."[3] The great circuit-riding preacher John Wesley's final words were, "The best of all is, God is with us. Farewell! Farewell!"[4] His brother Charles died talking to Jesus. "I shall be satisfied with Thy likeness—satisfied, satisfied."[5]

When someone is loved greatly, that person's final words become something to be treasured. So what of our beloved Lord Jesus's final words? Of course, every recorded word

Jesus spoke in His brief life on earth is of great value to us. We rightly study them. We parse and mine them for meaning. In them we seek direction for our lives and comfort for our souls—and never fail to find both.

Oh, but those lovely words gasped from that angry cross...those seven brief statements—one of them comprised only of two single-syllable words...those words uniquely distinguished by the unusual context in which they were uttered, so cherished beyond measure. They are rendered incalculably precious by the price He paid to utter them. We caught a fleeting glimpse of that price in the previous chapter. There we discovered that for a crucified man to speak anything at all from his torturous cross required almost unthinkable effort as a consequence of the compounding of pain upon pain. Surely these are words that merit our closest attention.

So, let us climb the craggy slope of Golgotha together again. Let us draw near to the cross and listen as we've never hearkened before. To realize it all will require that we stand there for six full hours—from about 9:00 a.m. to 3:00 p.m. with focused attention. The first half of that span we will stand in the full golden light of the Judean sun glistening against the backdrop of Jerusalem stone. Then suddenly the sun will seem to hide its face in sympathy over the agonizing cries of Jesus and leave us in virtual complete darkness for the last half. Across these hours we will hear the Savior speak a mere seven times.

He will have a word for His persecutors.

He will have a word for a penitent thief at His side.

Of course, there will be a word for His grief-shattered mother.

Then, after the sudden darkness at noon, three more words...crying, thirsting, and dying.

Then a final prayer, and it will be over.

THE FIRST WORD

Father, forgive them; for they know not what they do.
—LUKE 23:34

At long last, Jesus reaches Calvary. The feet that walked on Galilee's waters have willingly walked, stumbled, and even crawled to the site of suffering called The Skull. The hands that reached to bless countless seekers with healing and hope are now prepared to receive the massive nails.

The soldiers begin their cruel work. How well they know the process. The four-man team of Roman centurions has done this more times than they can count. All four are intoxicated, as usual. If a Roman soldier wasn't a heavy drinker before getting this worst of all assignments in this most strange and unglamorous of all Roman provinces, he certainly would be after a few weeks on the job. It was the only way to get through the blood-soaked, scream-filled days of anguish and woe.

Today there are only three scheduled for a long, slow execution—two common thieves and some rabble-rousing revolutionary who apparently got Himself on the wrong side of the local religious leaders. The thieves are first, and the nailing goes just as it always does. They resist initially, but the preceding flogging, by design, doesn't leave much fight in them. Once they are subdued, the swearing and cursing begin. These Roman soldiers have had the worst insults available hurled at them in a dozen different languages. And oh, what curses they have heard pronounced upon themselves. The names of various gods had been invoked to bring curses upon them, their bones, their loins, their families, and their children born and unborn. And these two thieves are no different. One of them in particular is quite passionate at spewing profanities and oaths at them.

With those two finally fastened to their crosses and hoisted skyward, it is time to deal with the Nazarene preacher. Surprisingly, He gives no resistance at all. Indeed, He seems to offer Himself willingly to the *Carnifix Serarum,* the Flesh Nailer. But the real shock comes a few moments later, after His cross is hoisted and the first of two spikes are about to be driven into His heels. They hear Him say something in Aramaic that begins with the word, "Abba." The soldiers spoke only Latin and a little Greek. But they recognize that word.

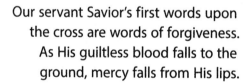

Our servant Savior's first words upon the cross are words of forgiveness. As His guiltless blood falls to the ground, mercy falls from His lips.

"Is He calling for His Father?" one of them asks. A Jewish bystander hears the exchange and offers some help. "He's praying for you. He asked God...He calls Him 'Father'...to not hold this against you...that you don't realize what you're doing. Come to think of it, He was probably praying for me too."

Of course. How could it have been any other way? Our servant Savior's first words upon the cross—spoken even as the nails were being driven deep into His flesh like fiery fangs—are words of forgiveness. As His guiltless blood falls to the ground, mercy falls from His lips. This is not what He simply said—this is who He supremely is. This He knows and He wants us to know...there is purpose in His pain. This is why He came. He Himself said it to the seeker Nicodemus who approached Him by night, "For God sent not his Son into the world to condemn the world; but that the world through him might be saved" (John 3:17).

Even now...especially now...our great High Priest is interceding. The soldiers hear it. The two thieves on His left and right hear it. The gathered onlookers hear it too. But most importantly, the Father hears it.

"Forgive them."

Clearly this petition for mercy extends beyond the soldiers simply doing their hellish duty like gentle ripples under the ocean of grace. It extends to the crowds who have cheered or jeered on this very day. It extends to those who conspired to bring it all about. But that prayer for mercy extends further still. That call for clemency expands to all...to every son and daughter of Adam's race in every age and in every place—to you and to me—and to all we sinners whose transgressions were the consummate cause that have now nailed the Son of God to Calvary's cross. Yes, He stands "in the gap" in that chasm constructed between Creator and creation. He alone upon two timbers has bridged that darkened abyss. He intercedes for us, whose sins He "bare...in his own body on the tree" (1 Peter 2:24).

Down...down through the corridors of time that fountain of forgiveness will flow to us. The headwaters of that river of mercy can be traced here—to the crest of this barren hill. This request of the Father was made here in this moment as His atoning blood begins to be shed...the first "word" from the cross...is Jesus giving voice to what His own spotless blood is asking...and still asks while these days of mercy continue. "Father, forgive them. They don't know what they do."

THE SECOND WORD

> Verily I say unto thee, To day shalt thou be with me in paradise.
>
> —LUKE 23:43

The midmorning sun still dares to look upon the scene unfolding on Golgotha. The silence of the Prince of God on the center cross stands in sharp relief and stark contrast to the hellish chorus of voices around Him.

There is the mockery and drunken shouting of the soldiers who, having divided up Jesus's belongings between them, are now in the midst of a raucous dice game to determine who was going to get the most prized article— His seamless tunic. There are the bellowing insults from the constant stream of passersby, moving in and out of the nearby gate to the city. The sign above the mutilated Messiah's head—"This is the King of the Jews"— provides fodder for an endless eruption of wisecracks. Then there are the representatives of the ruling religious authorities—the chief priest, the Sadducees, and the scribes who for months had nursed a seething, jealous hatred for the self-made and self-proclaimed rabbi from the backwoods of Nazareth. These took turns parading back and forth at the base of Jesus's cross hurling taunts: "He saved others; let him save himself, if he be Christ, the chosen of God" (Luke 23:35).

Eventually the clamoring chorus of abuse is joined from an unlikely quarter. It is one of the criminals being crucified beside the innocent Redeemer—the angry one. From His left Jesus hears, "So you're the Messiah, are you? Prove it by saving yourself—and us, too, while you're at it!" (Luke 23:39, NLT). The inflection and tone make it clear that this is a bitter taunt rather than a sincere plea for rescue. At this challenge, and all the rest, the Lamb of God remains silent. But unexpectedly, we hear a rebuke that comes from Jesus's right. It is the other thief. "Don't you fear God even when you have been sentenced to die? We deserve to die for our crimes, but this man hasn't done anything wrong" (Luke 23:40–41, NLT).

Even in this place and time of abuse and affliction, our great High Priest cannot leave a prayer for help unanswered. Even now, as forever through the ages, the feeblest cry of faith compels Him to rise up in response.

Clearly, something in Jesus's demeanor has convinced the man on His right hand that He was precisely who He said He was. Perhaps it was His grace and regal bearing under the crushing weight of pain and the incessant barrage of abuse. Maybe it was His earlier prayer for mercy for those who were inflicting that agony upon Him. Indeed, the sign nailed above His own head certainly spoke the truth. It said, "Thief." Why wouldn't the sign above Jesus's head be just as accurate? Perhaps this extraordinary man *is* "The King of the Jews," the very Son of God.

And so faith rises in a desperate man's heart, faith enough to prompt a plea: "Lord, remember me when thou comest into thy kingdom" (Luke 23:42).

Through every insult Calvary's Lamb had "opened not His mouth." Every challenge flung at Him had been ignored. No blasphemy merited a rebuke from His holy lips. But even in this place and time of abuse and affliction, our great High Priest cannot leave a prayer for help unanswered. Even now, as forever through the ages, the feeblest cry of faith compels Him to rise up in response.

"Verily, I say unto thee…"

Is it any wonder that Revelation 19:11 reveals His secret name to be "Faithful and True"? Jesus answers. And His affirmative response goes "exceeding abundantly beyond" what the dying thief could ask or think. He asks only to be "remembered." But Jesus says, "Today you will be with me in paradise."

Oh, what remarkable words these are…spoken in a moment such as this…to a man such as that. Can you imagine the quenching flood of peace and joy that rushed into the thirsty soul upon hearing that promise? He had been dragged to that tree a bitter reprobate. He had been bolted there a hopeless sinner. But with one simple prayer he became the first to discover a most glorious truth. It is a secret that Paul would proclaim a few decades later and that hundreds of millions across two millennia would realize for themselves: "Whosoever shall call upon the name of the Lord shall be saved" (Romans 10:13).

Today this penitent thief becomes the firstfruits of the great Emancipator's redemptive work, even while that work is underway.

Only a few days earlier Jesus had tried to warn His disciples of what was about to unfold and why it was necessary. He'd said, "And I, if I be lifted up from the earth, will draw all men unto me" (John 12:32).

Here, He has only been lifted up one hour, but with the second word from the cross, the magnetic power of Calvary's crucified Lamb is on display, and the drawing of sinners has already begun.

THE THIRD WORD

> Woman, behold thy son.... Behold thy mother!
> —JOHN 19:26–27

The sun is climbing higher. The Savior's strength is waning. As Jesus attempts to look down, His vision blurred by His swollen bleeding eyes, He sees a mob filled with hostile, hate-contorted faces. Amid that sea of scorn float two exceptions. In two pairs of eyes He finds only love and grief. And tears. One face belongs to His closest friend—John—"the disciple whom Jesus loved." When His eyes catch the other set of eyes and He looks into the other face, He sees a mother beholding something no mother should have to look upon. What she sees is unthinkable. Unbearable. But she has insisted on being here. Roman legions could not persuade her to leave. But the look Jesus sees on her face multiplies His pain. He has seen that look on a woman's face before.

Once, a year or so prior to this day, Jesus had encountered a funeral procession. A simple casket is flanked by a heartbroken widow woman. Years earlier she had lost her husband. And now she had lost her only son—her precious child and her only hope of being cared for in her old age. Jesus, moved with deep compassion for a shattered woman, halted that processional, touched the casket, and gave that mother back her son. Now, from the heights of the cross, He looks down into the face of a mother whose grief is far more profound. His compassion and affection for her are immense. But He cannot give her back her Son. He must not.

In these first hours on the cross
the living, dying Christ Jesus has
been the great intercessor.

So He fastens His eyes of perfect love upon her and kindly utters, "Woman, behold thy son!" He then directs His marred gaze to John as if to make it clear whom He means. We have heard Him call her "woman" before. It was three years ago, at that wedding in Cana. There she had drawn Him out—appealing to His compassion—to perform His first public miracle on behalf of a wedding couple facing potential humiliation.

He had protested then that His "time had not yet come." But now it has. So, looking to His most trusted disciple and friend, He completes the couplet: "Behold thy mother." When the Gospel of John is written many decades beyond this day, it will inform us: "And from that hour that disciple took her unto his own home." Of course, the writer would know. He was "that disciple."

In these first hours on the cross the living, dying Christ Jesus has been the great intercessor. He has interceded for those who were nailing Him to the cross. He has interceded for the repentant thief. And now He intercedes for His mother—the one who carried Him in her arms as an eight-day-old infant into the temple in Jerusalem to present Him to God. There in the temple courtyard she had encountered a silver-haired prophet named Simeon who, full of the Holy Ghost, rejoiced to have lived to see the arrival of the promised Messiah. The old man had prophesied over the child. He'd had a word of prophecy for the mother too. "And a sword will pierce your own soul," he had warned her.[6]

The day of that piercing has come. And suddenly the Palestinian sun refuses to beat upon His open wounds any longer, and the sun can bear to look no more.

THE FOURTH WORD

My God, my God, why hast thou forsaken me?
—MARK 15:34

The accumulated sin-guilt of fallen billions is being poured into and upon one guiltless man—not humanity deified or deity humanized. He was all God and He was all man. A holy God cannot be in contact with depravity and remain who He is. As Paul asked, "What fellowship has light with darkness?" (2 Corinthians 6:14, NAS). So, before the veil of the temple can be torn asunder, a heavy curtain must fall between the Father and the Son.

But now for this purpose for the first time, Jesus realizes that a man surrendered His position with the Father and only a man could purchase it back. So, as the warmth and light of the Father's countenance turns away from the Son, creation itself mirrors the abandonment. Deep darkness falls at noontime over Jerusalem. "He [God] made darkness his secret place; his pavilion round about him were dark waters and thick clouds of the skies" (Psalm 18:11). A hush now falls over the formerly raucous hillside. From this point forward, silence will govern these proceedings. The soldiers are out of jokes. They look warily at the sky and pull their crimson capes tight around them against the ill wind that now moans across the barren domed outcrop called Golgotha. Many of the religious elite suddenly remember something they need to attend to. The crowd thins.

More than one hundred years ago revivalist G. Campbell Morgan took a fresh look at the events of Good Friday and was struck by the significance of both the darkness and the silence:

> It is not to be passed over lightly that all the Synoptists record the fact of that darkness. Three hours of darkness and of silence! All the ribald clamor was over, the material opposition totally

exhausted, the turmoil ended. Man had done his last and his worst.... It is as though the appalling silence and that overwhelming darkness had changed the entire attitude of Man to the Savior.[7]

Something has changed. It is as if everyone present can sense a foundational and seismic shift in the state of the universe is in process. For nearly a full three hours—from noon to 3:00 p.m.—stillness stalks the stony place called The Skull. Then suddenly our attention is arrested by the man upon the center cross as He struggles to lift himself up to fill His blood-filled lungs with enough heavy air to wail something in Aramaic. It is the most pitiful cry anyone present has ever heard. From the eerie smothering silence, it echoes back from Jerusalem's walls and through the valley below.

Mark's Gospel's narrative of the life of Christ is unique in that it offers us numerous glimpses into Jesus's words in the Aramaic language that originally flowed from His lips. For example, according to Mark's account we know that when our Lord arrived, seemingly too late, at the deathbed of the young girl whose desperate father had begged Him to come, He said, "*Talitha cumi....*Damsel [little girl]...arise" (Mark 5:41).

Mark also tells us that as our Savior was impaled upon the stake, He cried out, "*Eloi, Eloi, lama sabach-thani?...*My God, my God, why hast thou forsaken me?" (Mark 15:34).

In chapter 2 we observed that this is not actually an expression of surprise. The dying Son of God is not bewildered. He is doing what He had always done in moments of stress or spiritual warfare. He is quoting Scripture—in this case, Psalm 22:1. Among the middle verses of this most descriptive psalm we find this:

> I am poured out like water, and all my bones are out of joint: my heart is like wax; it is melted in the midst of my bowels. My strength is dried up like a potsherd; and my tongue cleaveth to my jaws; and thou hast brought me into the dust of death. For dogs have compassed me: the assembly of the wicked have enclosed me: they pierced my hands and my feet. I may tell all my bones: they look and stare upon me. They part my garments among them, and cast lots upon my vesture.
>
> —PSALM 22:14–18

Is it any wonder Jesus had this particular psalm on His mind? He was experiencing it verse by devastating verse! The psalmist David had prophetically looked down through the centuries and for a brief, terrifying moment been granted a look through the eyes of his descendant upon the cross.

"My God, my God, why hast thou forsaken me?" This is not actually an expression of surprise. The dying Son of God is not bewildered.

Jesus had this psalm engraved upon the fleshly tablet of His heart, and He knew this moment of absolute

85

abandonment would come. Indeed, the anticipation of it contributed to His profound despair and near-panic in the Garden of Gethsemane only a few hours earlier. Nevertheless, it was a shock to the Son's battered soul and psyche to experience the Father's necessary withdrawal of His presence. And so...

> And at the ninth hour Jesus cried with a loud voice, saying, *Eloi, Eloi, lama sabachthani?* which is, being interpreted, My God, my God, why hast thou forsaken me?
>
> —MARK 15:34

THE FIFTH WORD

> I thirst.
>
> —JOHN 19:28

He who is living water personified is dying of thirst.

It has been twenty-four hours since He had a scrap of bread or a drop of water. He suffers from massive blood loss and a well-understood physiological phenomenon associated with severe injury—shock. Anyone who has been through a basic first aid course knows that two things are immediately called for when an injured person goes into shock—warmth and water. God's only begotten Son is naked and thirsty. And death is circling near. He has hung suspended between heaven and earth for six excruciating hours now. The Lamb's work of atonement is close to its conclusion. And so He can now request and accept what He had earlier refused—life-giving, comforting water.

After this, Jesus knowing that all things were now accomplished, that the scripture might be fulfilled, saith, I thirst.

—JOHN 19:28

This simple two-word statement is a jarring reminder that this Jesus, though fully God, is very much one of us in every conceivable way. He has laid aside every divine privilege and prerogative to walk here among us and accomplish what was legally necessary to restore that which was lost to us back in the garden.

He is fully man. He feels what we feel. He needs what we need. He thirsts.

As we hear this pitiful plea, more croaked across His swollen parched throat than spoken, we recall another day in which He asked for water. On that hot afternoon at a Samarian well He requested a drink of a woman who came to draw there. He violated both social convention and strict religious law by merely making eye contact. Then He asked her for some water.

> How much do we do without…how much grace, help, and favor do we forgo…simply because we've lost sight of Calvary's crucified Lamb.

Feisty and hardened by a life filled with wrong choices and wrong men, she wanted to debate. He wanted to change her life. He said:

> If you knew the gift of God, and who it is who says
> to you, "Give Me a drink," you would have asked
> Him, and He would have given you living water.
> —JOHN 4:10, NKJV

Here lies a lifetime's worth of spiritual wisdom embedded in this brief statement.

If you knew who...

You would have asked...

And He would have given...

The more we come to understand the "who" of Jesus— the depth of His love, the breadth of His atoning work— the bolder we grow in asking of Him. How much do we do without...how much grace, help, and favor do we forgo...simply because we've lost sight of Calvary's crucified Lamb.

When asked by the woman about that mysterious "living water," Jesus explained:

> Whoever drinks of this water will thirst again, but
> whoever drinks of the water that I shall give him
> will never thirst. But the water that I shall give him
> will become in him a fountain of water springing up
> into everlasting life.
> —JOHN 4:13–14, NKJV

That was then. Today the One who will one day send the Comforter to us can receive no comfort in this place. When He requests a little water, He receives bitter vinegar.

> Now there was set a vessel full of vinegar: and they
> filled a sponge with vinegar, and put it upon hyssop,
> and put it to his mouth.
> —JOHN 19:29

We should note that the Gospel narrative says Jesus only dared to say "I thirst" because He knew "all things" had now been "accomplished."

Here at the foot of His cross the spirit realm is invisible to our natural eyes. We've seen a man suffering. What we have not witnessed is what has transpired in the unseen realm. So let us now look not at the things that are seen but at the things that cannot be seen. We must look beyond this scene to the unseen. By so doing, we can see what we could not—the hordes of grotesque, gleeful, and giddy demons who have finally seen the lowering of the hedge of protection that always surrounded heaven's Prince. He was finally vulnerable to torment and attack.

It's been eerily dark and quiet on Golgotha for three hours now. It would be easy to assume that nothing of significance has transpired. But in that same span, in the great court of heaven has been the scene of a remarkable flurry of activity. Legal processes have been executed…accounting has been done…business has been transacted. A kinsman redeemer has stepped forward to pay the necessary price to redeem an enslaved relative—Adam and his every willing descendant. A long-open set of accounting books has been reconciled and closed. A cosmic stamp pounds an ancient page, leaving behind a blood-red message across the writing there. "Paid in Full."

Only now can a sixth word from that grisly cross be uttered. It comes quickly.

THE SIXTH WORD

It is finished.

—JOHN 19:30

It is an exclamation of the very Godhead—three in one.

A corner has been turned. A goal has been reached, a mountain climbed, an ocean crossed, a valley transversed, a foe conquered, a victory won, and a king crowned. The suffocating blanket of darkness that has covered the last half of these proceedings begins to lift. Now that the sun can once again be discerned, we realize it has already begun its fiery plunge into the Mediterranean to be extinguished for another night. The Jewish Sabbath rest begins at sundown, and it is rapidly approaching.

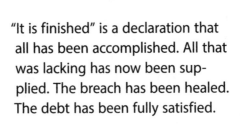

"It is finished" is a declaration that all has been accomplished. All that was lacking has now been supplied. The breach has been healed. The debt has been fully satisfied.

The few remaining observers on Golgotha heard the man on the center cross shout something about His God having abandoned Him. A little later He had whispered a request for water—one that was answered, not with a ladle of cooling, soothing water but with a vinegar-filled sponge. Now we see the expiring troubadour of heaven summoning His last remnants of physical and mental strength...rising to speak once more.

Just one word this time.

When John, the beloved disciple, recalls this statement to record it in his Gospel narrative, he uses a Greek accounting term—*tetelestai*.[8] Future English translations of John's Gospel will render that term in a way that tends to strip it of the legal and financial connotations. They translate it, "It is finished" (three words for one). But *tetelestai* does not mean merely that a thing has ended. It has a far greater implication than merely a clock has run out and the game has concluded. It is a declaration that all has been accomplished. All that was lacking has now been supplied. The breach has been healed. The debt has been fully satisfied. Shalom—nothing broken, nothing missing.

Charles Spurgeon called this declaration, "Christ's dying word to the church." But our King's proclamation carries even more dimensions of meaning than this. He means that all the types, shadows, and symbols of the Old Testament have now been fully manifested in Him. He decrees that the prophecies that pointed to a future Deliverer King have been fulfilled. John the Baptist had asked, "Are you the One or should we look for another?" Jesus's answer at that time was suggestive but indirect. Now He speaks plainly. His *"Tetelestai!"* emphatically shouts, "You can stop looking! The promised One has appeared and accomplished the prophesied task. Dominion of planet Earth has been restored to its rightful steward."

As Spurgeon wrote of this victory cry:

> [T]he whole Book, from the first to the last, in both the Law and the Prophets, was finished in Him! There is not a single jewel of promise, from the first emerald which fell on the threshold of Eden, to the last sapphire of Malachi which was not set in the breastplate of the true High Priest. No, there is not a type, from the red heifer downward to the turtle dove, from the hyssop upwards to Solomon's

> Temple itself, which was not fulfilled in Him; and
> not a prophecy, whether spoken on Chebar's bank
> or on the shores of Jordan; not a dream of wise
> men, whether they had received it in Babylon, or
> in Samaria, or in Judea, which was not now fully
> worked out in Christ Jesus![9]

Finally, in that cry of consummation, Jesus declared an end to separated man's religious striving to build a ladder back to God. God Himself has donned flesh and bone and blood and condescended to fallen men and willingly lain down on a cross.

"It is finished!" we hear Him cry aloud. Then He slowly, reverently, and with victorious humility bows that thorn-pierced head. Yes, of course, He bows now. There is nothing left to do but exhale a prayer.

THE SEVENTH WORD

> Father, into thy hands I commend my spirit.
> —LUKE 23:46

In a sense, the final words of the Savior upon the cruel beam are a mirror of His first recorded words.

It was the excellent historian Luke who mined mother Mary's memories about the young Messiah and learned of a day—twenty-one Passovers ago, this very weekend—in which two worried parents found the twelve-year-old Jesus missing from their caravan of Jerusalem pilgrims.

An agonizing three-day search of the crowded, labyrinthine city finally revealed the boy sitting in the courtyard of the temple dazzling the Jewish scholars and teachers with His understanding of the Scriptures. A frantic Mary scolded Him well for putting her and Joseph through the worry and effort of the investigation. The Son, on the doorstep of the milestone thirteenth birthday for a Jewish boy, expresses surprise that they didn't know exactly where He would be: "Did you not know that I must be about My Father's business?" (Luke 2:49, NKJV).

> Jesus must of His own human volition agree to die, or we would have nothing more than a murdered sacrifice.

Upon reaching the significant milestone age of thirty, He put His hand to His Father's business in earnest. Now, on this day of betrayal, suffering, isolation, and grief—in the shadow of that same temple—He has been about His Father's business once more. It is the business of restoring a lost, fallen, and depraved race to fellowship with the God they had insulted, abandoned, and betrayed. It is the culmination of a business plan thousands of years in the execution. Now the Son's portion of the Father's business is complete.

The next step, bringing the Son back from death, is in the Father's hands. But this will only be necessary if the Son chooses willingly to submit Himself to death's domain. Jesus must of His own human volition agree to die, or we would have nothing more than a murdered sacrifice. He could still choose to leap free from that wooden beam upon which He had been bolted. He could still summon the angelic hosts who were standing at attention with swords already drawn from their sheaths. Death has neither power nor authority to take Him against His will.

So "with a loud voice," as though to gain His Father's attention, He speaks His final words this side of the empty tomb. With all His remaining strength He shouts a prayer of consecration. "Father, into Your hands I commend My spirit!" It is an expression of trust, of faith in a Father whose abiding presence He can no longer feel or sense. He is saying, "If I surrender Myself to death's icy embrace here, I am placing My trust in You not to leave Me in his noxious, toxic, venomous grasp."

He is in essence saying, "Father, I know Your Holy Spirit will not leave My body in that cold tomb because in a few years a preacher named Paul needs to be able to write to My friends and say: 'But if the Spirit of him that raised up Jesus from the dead dwell in you, he that raised up Christ from the dead shall also quicken your mortal bodies by his Spirit that dwelleth in you.'"[10]

Jesus is saying, "You will not leave Me here, Father, because a thousand years ago the psalmist David prophetically looked down through the ages, saw a stone-sealed tomb, and wrote on behalf of the sacrificed Lamb: 'For thou wilt not leave my soul in hell; neither wilt thou suffer thine Holy One to see corruption.'[11]

"You will not leave Me in death's grip, Father, because fifty days from this day My friend Simon Peter, who only a few hours ago denied he even knew Me, is going to be a new, Holy Ghost–filled man. And he is going to stand up in front of all of Jerusalem and preach the first Spirit-filled sermon, shouting:

"'Men of Israel, hear these words: Jesus of Nazareth, a Man attested by God to you by miracles, wonders, and signs which God did through Him in your midst, as you yourselves also know—Him, being delivered by the determined purpose and foreknowledge of God, you have taken by lawless hands, have crucified, and put to death; whom God raised up, having loosed the pains of death, because it was not possible that He should be held by it.'"[13]

Even here at Golgotha amid the smell, sight, and sound of suffering flesh and dying shame, He is still about His Father's business. So, He dies praying: "Father, into Your hands I commend My spirit!"

He prays that word of prayer and dies...so that you and I might pray it also and live.

THE EXCHANGE
AT THE CROSS

Chapter 5

*When Christ died He left a will in which He
gave His soul to His Father, His body to Joseph
of Arimathea, His clothes to the soldiers, and
His mother to John. But to His disciples, who
had left all to follow Him, He left not silver or
gold, but something far better—His PEACE!*[1]
—MATTHEW HENRY
(1662–1714)

I T IS 1626, and Henry Hudson's Dutch West India
Company has its eye on a rocky, tree-covered little
island on the northeastern coast of what will one day
be called the United States of America. No Native American tribes reside permanently on the oblong, twenty-two-
square-mile parcel at this time. However, the Lenape tribe
does utilize it as a seasonal hunting and fishing ground.
They call it "island of many hills," or in the Lenape tongue,
manna-hatta.

The Dutch West India Company dispatches Peter
Minuit to broker a deal with the Lenape Indians. In
exchange for what would one day be called the island of

Manhattan, Minuit offered the tribe a large chest of beads and trinkets.[2]

Now it is 1867, and an all-night session of negotiations between the United States and Russia has resulted in a bleary-eyed 4:00 a.m. treaty signing. The Russians have agreed to sell all 586,412 square miles of the territory called Alaska to the United States for the purchase price of $7.2 million. In other words, America got one of the largest, most beautiful, and resource-rich pieces of planet Earth for two cents per acre.[3]

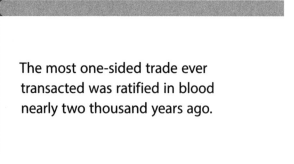

The most one-sided trade ever transacted was ratified in blood nearly two thousand years ago.

It is 1919, and the Boston Red Sox are the perennial kings of major league baseball—winning championship after championship. Their star player is unhappy, so they sell him to the nearby team that is the perennial cellar dweller in the league—the New York Yankees. Babe Ruth becomes a Yankee, and the Red Sox will not see another championship for more than eighty-five years as they watch the Yankees become the most storied and successful club of the twentieth century, appearing in forty World Series championships and winning twenty-seven of them.[4]

These are examples of some of the best trades in history (or worst, depending upon which side of the trade you were standing on). But the most one-sided trade ever transacted was ratified in blood nearly two thousand years ago. This appallingly lopsided agreement was entered into not because one of the parties was unknowing or foolish or gullible. No, in this case unequaled and unconditional love drove the generous party to the bargaining table—a love so profound that one day Paul will pray that somehow you and I might be able to "comprehend with all saints what is the breadth, and length, and depth, and height" of that love (Ephesians 3:18). The covenant was between God and His Son—perfection with perfection—not God and us. The cross of Christ is the spiritually legal trading table at which every one of us is offered an opportunity to make an extraordinary set of exchanges. There are seven trades in particular that make the invitation at Calvary the most one-sided offer ever extended. Indeed it would seem too good to be true had these seven offers not come from One who is indeed only incapable of deceit. And if I, along with a billion others down through the centuries, hadn't experienced these wondrous exchanges firsthand, they could appear as Moses declaring Israel's exodus from Egypt—but a mocking dream. "When the LORD turned again the captivity of Zion, we were like them that dreamed a dream" (Psalm 126:1).

THE FIRST EXCHANGE: OUR SINFULNESS FOR HIS RIGHTEOUSNESS

> For he hath made him to be sin for us, who knew
> no sin; that we might be made the righteousness of
> God in him.
>
> —2 CORINTHIANS 5:21

Our pristine parents chose the wrong tree. Adam and Eve believed what is literally and verifiably the oldest lie in the book—"you shall be like God." Against the explicit instructions of a benevolent Father-Creator, they partook of the fruit of the tree of the knowledge of good and evil. And innocence died.

Prior to that day man and God were one. Adam fellowshipped freely with his Father in the pristine brilliance of paradise. Their relationship was one of unguarded openness. There were no reassurances needed. With the breezes of eternity blowing cool around his mortal shoulders, he hears these whispered words: "Who shall separate me from the love of God?"

Then...right there in the middle of paradise...Adam sided with God's great archenemy, and in that very moment a great creeping sickness entered his soul. The tree's promise of the knowledge of good and evil was indeed fulfilled, with catastrophic effect. A knowledge of every evil atrocity and abomination filled and flooded his being, as well as an acute awareness of everything good that lay just beyond his sin-infected reach.

In the fresh hollowness of his heart man hears these words: "Blessed are the pure in heart, for they alone shall see God." But the pure had become polluted. Man had successfully separated himself from his friend, and a huge gulf now separated Creator and creation. One exposure to Satan's corruption carried the communicable disease of sin and infiltrated the bloodstream of all humanity.

What is this thing that has such awful ability to separate God and Creator from man and creation? What is it that formed this chasm? What could possibly have been so strong and mighty, so dark and drastic as to have driven a wedge between a timeless God and a temporal man?

It is sin. And from the womb we suffer under its congenital effects. It separates our hearts from His heart. It causes us to go left when we know we should go right. It's what makes us accept the counterfeit as real and reject the real as counterfeit. It drives us to our own destruction. It makes us say what we shouldn't want to say, and go where we shouldn't want to go, and do what we shouldn't want to do. It compels us to hurt, use, and abuse the very ones we should love and serve.

But when we approach the cross we find an offer waiting. There, a perfectly righteous (in right standing with God) Man—one whose blood had never been infected by Adam's contagious, infectious disease of alienation from God—hangs willing to make an exchange with us.

"Give Me your sinfulness," He says. "I'll give you My righteousness."

Isaiah prophetically looked forward through the halls of history, saw that cross, and cried, "The LORD has laid on Him the iniquity of us all" (Isaiah 53:6, NKJV). The apostle Peter could look back at the cross and say, "Who his own self bare our sins in his own body on the tree, that we, being dead to sins, should live unto righteousness"

(1 Peter 2:24). And John, the one who was chosen to be Jesus's own mother's security escort at her Son's execution on the tree, looked back at that daunting day and could only utter, "This is real love—not that we loved God, but that he loved us and sent his Son as a sacrifice to take away our sins" (1 John 4:10, NLT).

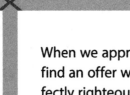

> When we approach the cross we find an offer waiting. There, a perfectly righteous Man hangs willing to make an exchange with us.

Indeed, only real love would offer such a trade. Jesus takes not only our individual acts of sin but also our *sinfulness*—that disease we inherited from our earthly forefather Adam. In exchange He imparts to us His own righteousness, and with it the ability to enjoy that communion and connectedness to God that Adam forfeited.

Jesus was made sin with our sinfulness that we might be made righteous with His righteousness. This is the first exchange available at the cross. It is an astonishing trade, but it is far from the only one available there.

THE SECOND EXCHANGE: OUR SHAME FOR HIS GLORY

> And the LORD God called unto Adam, and said unto him, Where art thou? And he said, I heard thy voice in the garden, and I was afraid, because I was naked; and I hid myself.
>
> —GENESIS 3:9–10

The primal evidence of mankind's plummet from grace was the presence of shame. It manifested in the first couple's fear-soaked shrinking from the presence of God. The sound of His footfalls had only the previous day filled their hearts with joy and caused them to come running to meet Him in glad anticipation. Now His footsteps filled them with dread. Their Father God had not changed. But they had.

"I was afraid."

"Because I was naked."

"And I hid myself."

Shame had wrapped its suffocating tentacles of degradation around their souls. So the first couple hastily contrived, through a newly depraved intellect and irreversibly warped ability to reason, a fear-based and flawed attempt to cloak their remorse, regret, and self-reproach. Religion was born. Over the subsequent millennia the sons of Adam and the daughters of Eve would devise ever more clever and sophisticated ways to try to cover that shame. But "cover" was the best they could do.

In the Old Testament we find two key Hebrew words for "shame"—and they communicate two very different concepts. The word *bosheth* connotes the guilt and dishonor we experience when our sin is exposed. Daniel used this word when he said, "Righteousness belongs to You, O Lord, but to us, open shame..." (Daniel 9:7, NAS). It is *bosheth*, in part, that drove Adam and Eve to flee the holy presence of God. And every person alive has experienced its sting.

There is another Hebrew word for a very different type of pain—one that is also usually translated "shame" or "ashamed" in our English Bibles. It is *kalam*, and it speaks of being hurt, rejected, insulted, disgraced, defiled, or humiliated—usually in public and particularly by someone close to you. To understand the concept of *kalam*, all that is necessary is a glance at Numbers 12:14 (emphasis added):

> And the LORD said unto Moses, If her father had but spit in her face, should she not be *ashamed* seven days?

This is *kalam*—a man spitting in his own daughter's face. Imagine a lovely Israelite girl being brought before the elders of her tribe for some perceived breach of custom. It's all a misunderstanding. She has done nothing wrong. But with the entire village watching, her angry and embarrassed father does not rise to her defense. Instead he walks up to her and spits in her face. Her face flushes red and tears fill her eyes. What she feels in that moment is *kalam*.

We know the shame of the other type—*bosheth*—well. It's that sense of uncleanness we feel when we sin—when we violate God's immutable laws—resulting in damage to ourselves or others. Its close companion is our English word *guilt*.

But we all are far, far too familiar with that second type of shame as well. We are intimately acquainted with that humiliating sense of defilement and worthlessness we sense when others use or abuse us. Every wife who has suffered the fist of a drunken husband knows this shame. So does every victim of rape. Every violated little boy or girl knows it too, as does every girl ever pressured by a parent or a boyfriend to abort the growing new life in her womb. Every man who has endured the living hell of learning from a friend about his wife's infidelity has felt it.

"This was your fault," the adversary of your soul whispers. "You provoked this. You deserved this. You're not worth any more than this." And to the post-Edenic soul...to the heart that has not been to Calvary to make the great exchange and witnessed the staggering price God Almighty was willing to pay to reclaim it...these lies seem to carry the nauseating ring of truth.

Put simply, we feel the first shame when we hurt someone else. We feel the second when someone hurts us. And the very history of the human race since the Fall is little more than these two forms of shame dancing across the ravaged souls of men and women. Abusing and being abused. Defiling and being defiled.

Hurt people hurting people.

All the crushing burden of shame our Savior bore upon His back to that wooden beam. With this awful truth in mind, observe with fresh eyes Hebrews 12:2: "Looking unto Jesus the author and finisher of our faith; who for the joy that was set before him *endured the cross, despising the shame,* and is set down at the right hand of the throne of God" (emphasis added).

When the living Christ Jesus looked ahead to the cross, He didn't see only pain. He saw unspeakable shame— our shame, both *bosheth* and *kalam,* being heaped upon Himself in almost infinite measure. Only looking beyond that shame to the joy of being "the firstborn of many brethren" could propel Him forward in obedience into that abyss.

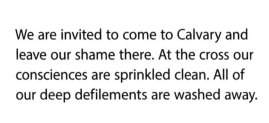

We are invited to come to Calvary and leave our shame there. At the cross our consciences are sprinkled clean. All of our deep defilements are washed away.

Oh, what shame Jesus bore on that Friday. Over and over they spit upon His blessed face during that mockery of a trial. He was stripped naked, exposed, and hung in humiliation before demons, before men, and before His Father. And in the unseen realm, the bloodguiltiness of every sinner was laid like a lodestone upon His conscience.

One of the great glories of the cross is that Jesus did more than bear our sin. He bore the first great consequence of sin—our shame. No matter what we've done or what has been done to us, we are invited to come to Calvary and leave our shame there. At the cross our consciences are sprinkled clean. All of our deep defilements are washed away.

In one of the most astonishing of exchanges ever proposed, we are invited to trade our shame for His glory. It is, therefore, no wonder that the Book of Revelation reveals Jesus enthroned in that glory declaring, "Behold, I make all things new" (Revelation 21:5).

THE THIRD EXCHANGE: OUR CURSE FOR HIS BLESSING

> Christ hath redeemed us from the curse of the law,
> being made a curse for us: for it is written, Cursed
> is every one that hangeth on a tree.
>
> —GALATIANS 3:13

It is of utmost importance to understand that phrase, "the curse of the law." The law—the code of God's immutable principles, character, and precepts woven into the very fabric of the universe—is not and never was a curse. It was the *violation* of that law that unleashed a curse upon creation. God had delegated dominion authority to man. And man, like Esau, had sold his birthright to satisfy a craving.

Humanity was created to live in blessing. In fact, the twenty-eighth chapter of Deuteronomy promises fourteen extravagant blessings to those who obey His commands. However, it also outlines fifty-four curses to those who fail to keep the Lord's statutes. Some may interpret this to mean that God is more interested in cursing us than blessing us, but alas, that couldn't be further from the truth. In reality, He is simply revealing everything He has delivered us out of and kept us from!

The garden in which the Creator placed Adam and Eve was a place of abundance and blessing. Indeed, in the first chapter of the first book of the Bible, the first declaration we hear the Creator speaking over our ancestors are words of blessing:

> *And God blessed them*, and God said unto them, Be
> fruitful, and multiply, and replenish the earth, and
> subdue it: and have dominion over the fish of the

sea, and over the fowl of the air, and over every
living thing that moveth upon the earth.

—GENESIS 1:28,

EMPHASIS ADDED

When man forfeited that delegated dominion to a
deceiving usurper, he set free a curse upon the earth in place
of that blessing. Sickness, poverty, jealousy, rage, decay, and
death permeated a once-perfect system. The very ground
itself became cursed—refusing to complacently yield provision and bounty. For earth's first couple and for every man,
woman, and child who would follow after them, pain, diffi-
culty, and hardship became constant companions.

As God delivers the crushing news about this curse, He
inserts a note of hope and promise. As He pronounces the
implications of the curse upon the tempter-serpent, God
adds: "And I will put enmity between thee and the woman,
and between thy seed and her seed; it shall bruise thy head,
and thou shalt bruise his heel" (Genesis 3:15).

The scarlet thread of redemption begins here with
that promised "Seed" and ends at a thorn-pierced brow
on Golgotha. In between it runs through a man named
Abram who also receives a promise about that coming
"Seed"—namely that in Him "shall all the nations of the
earth be blessed." Yes, *blessed*. When that Seed comes, the
reign of the curse will be ended. Blessedness will return to
the human family.

The first Adam let this curse loose in the world. At the
cross the last Adam established the legal framework for
turning blessing loose in its place:

> Christ hath redeemed us from the curse of the law,
> being made a curse for us: for it is written, Cursed

is every one that hangeth on a tree: *That the blessing of Abraham* might come on the Gentiles through Jesus Christ; that we might receive the promise of the Spirit through faith.

—GALATIANS 3:13–14,

EMPHASIS ADDED

Do you see it? At the cross we can exchange life under Adam's curse for Abraham's life of blessing. In the last chapter of the last book of the Bible, John is given a glimpse of the day when the full implications of that victory are in effect across the earth. John looks at that hour and writes, "And there shall be no more curse..." (Revelation 22:3).

Until that day arrives, we can still personally and individually experience redemption from the curse, made possible through an exchange at the curse-eradicating cross of Christ.

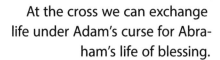

At the cross we can exchange life under Adam's curse for Abraham's life of blessing.

THE FOURTH EXCHANGE: OUR BROKENNESS FOR HIS HEALING

But he was wounded for our transgressions, he was bruised for our iniquities: the chastisement of our

peace was upon him; and with his stripes we are
healed.

—ISAIAH 53:5

Here, in Isaiah's great prophetic exposition of the suffering Messiah, the language of substitution and exchange
is abundant and explicit. *He* receives wounds for *our*
transgressions. *He* receives bruises for *our* iniquities.
Our peace is purchased by *His* chastisement. *His* stripes—
inflicted by the centurion's nine-stranded whip—effected
our healing.

Prior to Adam's great fall, the garden was a place where
the blighted foot of sickness and disease had never trod.
Part of the devastating fallout of Adam's forfeiture of
earth's stewardship was rampant disease, deformity, and
infirmity. Pain and pestilence were not a part of the perfect handiwork that God declared "good." Sickness was
and is a work of the enemy; thus Peter's sermon in Acts
recalls, "How God anointed Jesus of Nazareth with the
Holy Ghost and with power: who went about doing good,
and healing all that were oppressed of the devil" (Acts
10:38). Throughout Scripture, disease is associated with
the demonic works of darkness.

Jesus came to "destroy the works of the devil" (1 John
3:8). The last Adam came to restore what the first Adam
had lost.

Nevertheless, through the centuries since that Good
Friday, there have always been those who—for whatever
reason—have chosen to believe that no provision for physical healing was made in the atoning work of Christ. And
not surprisingly, such believers have seen little in the way
of Jesus's healing virtue flowing in their lives.

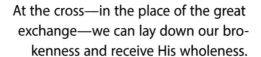

At the cross—in the place of the great exchange—we can lay down our brokenness and receive His wholeness.

In contrast, wherever there has been intellectual honesty and scriptural accuracy...wherever the truth of Calvary has been preached...wherever Isaiah 53 has been read in the revealing light of the cross...there have been those who have come to that bloody beam and exchanged their brokenness—spiritual, physical, and emotional—for God's wholeness. Innumerable sick and suffering children of God have walked boldly into the court of heaven and there presented Isaiah 53:5 and 1 Peter 2:24 as legal documents establishing their biblical right to healing, and walked out whole...nothing missing, nothing broken.

Jesus once told a desperate father seeking healing for his child, "If thou canst believe, all things are possible to him that believeth" (Mark 9:23). That man walked away hand in hand with a son who was whole and free. In the same way, those faith-filled souls who come to the cross believing that there Jesus bore their sicknesses, carried their pains, and by His stripes they were healed—they walk away changed as well.

There—in the place of the great exchange—they lay down their brokenness and receive His wholeness.

THE FIFTH EXCHANGE:
OUR POVERTY FOR HIS ABUNDANCE

> For ye know the grace of our Lord Jesus Christ, that,
> though he was rich, yet for your sakes he became
> poor, that ye through his poverty might be rich.
> —2 CORINTHIANS 8:9

In recent years great debates have roiled certain segments
of the American church over the question of whether Jesus
was poor or wealthy. It seems some people need a poor
Jesus or a rich Jesus, depending upon which one better
serves the needs of their theology or personal experience.

Laying aside the question of Jesus's financial standing
during His life and ministry, the verse quoted above,
2 Corinthians 8:9, explicitly states that Jesus "became"
poor at some point in order to effect yet another aspect of
the great exchange.

In truth, Jesus *became* poor in two key senses. First, He
became poor in relative terms the moment He stepped out
of heavenly eternity and stepped into the body of a man.
He laid aside the splendor of heaven's throne and moved
into the vulnerable, fragile body of an infant lying in a
feed trough in a rustic desert village in the Middle East.
It's hard to view that as anything but a significant step
down in lifestyle.

Indeed, it stands as the most radical drop in status,
privilege, and comfort any resident of the universe has
ever willingly chosen. Paul clearly had this truth in mind
when he wrote:

> Have this attitude in yourselves which was also in
> Christ Jesus, who, although He existed in the form

of God, did not regard equality with God a thing to be grasped [clung to], but emptied Himself, taking the form of a bond-servant...

—PHILIPPIANS 2:5–7, NAS

> Jesus became poor so that destitute paupers like you and me could become living heirs of the King of glory.

We don't know how much money was in that treasury box the pilfering Judas used to carry around. We do know, however, that whatever Jesus accumulated in His life was stripped from Him at Golgotha. As He stood before Pilate, nothing remained in the possession of the Prince of God but the robe upon His back, some physical strength, and His dignity. Soon all of these would be ripped away from Him as well. The once-and-future King hung naked and despised before a watching world as Roman soldiers gambled for His tunic.

Never has a man been so utterly destitute as was Jesus on that hill in those final moments. He became poor in every way a person can be poor. He had no possessions, no comfort, no defenders, and no friends, save beloved John. Why? So that destitute paupers like you and me could become living heirs of the King of glory.

When we approach the cross and accept the terms of the great exchange, we become rich in love, rich in hope, rich in peace, rich in power, and yes, rich in abundant provision for our every material need.

The centrality of the cross is the hallmark of an authentic, life-giving gospel—a gospel with the power to heal not only the sin-sick, heartbroken individual but also entire cultures.

THE SIXTH EXCHANGE: OUR REJECTION FOR HIS ACCEPTANCE

> But now in Christ Jesus you who formerly were far off have been brought near by the blood of Christ.
> —EPHESIANS 2:13, NAS

The first man and woman took one last backward look at what had been the only home they'd ever known. And what a home it had been. Plenty and peace, purpose and provision had characterized their every moment in Eden.

Their rebellion and the resulting curse they loosed upon the world had made their banishment from paradise necessary. But the worst of it wasn't the loss of abundance and comfort...as awful and pitiful as that was. The most devastating aspect of Adam's treason was the loss of intimacy with the Father Creator. Adam, Eve, and a thousand generations of progeny—including you and me—would be alienated from the loving Father. They had been created explicitly for fellowship, but now they were no longer capable of engaging in direct contact with God. Indeed, they weren't even capable of surviving it...as the pure fire of a holy God's glory would have destroyed man in his fallen state.

We're told that God spoke to Moses as a man speaks to a friend. Yet even Moses had to be hidden in the cleft of a rock if he were to survive even a moment of proximity to His Majesty. From that day of exile forward, alienation became endemic in all human relationships. Misunderstanding, mistrust, jealousy, envy, betrayal, and loneliness now sat upon the throne of every heart.

Who among us doesn't bear the invisible wounds and scars of being rejected by others? In self-defense we learn early to reject others before we have the opportunity to be rejected by them.

Even so, in reality the greatest source of pain for every lost soul that has not found its way to Calvary, whether they consciously realize it or not, is their sense of separation from the heart of the Abba of Jesus. As seventeenth-century mathematician Blaise Pascal said, "There was once in man a true happiness of which there now remain in him only the mark and empty trace...because the infinite abyss can only be filled by an infinite and immutable object, that is to say, only by God Himself."[5] Paraphrased, this can read, "There is a God-shaped vacuum in the heart of every man which cannot be filled by any created thing, but only by God, the Creator, made known through Jesus." Paul described it in terms of alienation. "Having the understanding darkened, being *alienated* from the life of God...," he writes concerning fallen people in Ephesians 4:18. Of course, Paul knew the only remedy for that separation from God's life and presence was to come to the cross and make an exchange. At Calvary Jesus takes our rejection and alienation from God, taking it upon Himself. In exchange He offers us the complete and utter acceptance by the Father that was uniquely His.

In other words, our alienation from God was nailed to the cross of Christ. This is why Paul is able to write:

> And you, that were sometime alienated and enemies in your mind by wicked works, yet now hath he reconciled in the body of his flesh through death, to present you holy and unblameable and unreproveable in his sight.
>
> —COLOSSIANS 1:21–22

Why was rejection by men and isolation from God such a key part of our Lord's experience on the stake? Because He was our substitute. He suffered our deep rejection so that we can now enjoy His acceptance.

When Isaiah got a prophetic glimpse of the crucified King on that cruel cross, this is what he saw: "He is despised and rejected of men; a man of sorrows, and acquainted with grief: and we hid as it were our faces from him; he was despised, and we esteemed him not" (Isaiah 53:3). Jesus Christ is "the stone which the builder's rejected."[6] Speaking of Himself in the third person, Jesus told His disciples, "He must suffer many things and be rejected by this generation" (Luke 17:25, NKJV).

Why was rejection by men and isolation from God such a key part of our Lord's experience on the stake? Because He was our substitute. He suffered our deep rejection so that we can now enjoy His acceptance. It is so we can come to God, not as groveling servants but as welcomed sons and daughters. It is to make it possible and natural and appropriate for us to boldly approach the throne of grace to find help in time of need.

This is why the veil of the temple was torn asunder at the moment Jesus exhaled His last breath. The way back to Eden—back to God's fellowship and presence—was open once more.

Our doorway home is shaped like a cross.

THE SEVENTH EXCHANGE: OUR DEATH FOR HIS LIFE

> For the wages of sin is *death*; but the gift of God is eternal *life* through Jesus Christ our Lord.
> —ROMANS 6:23, EMPHASIS ADDED

An historian of ancient Greece records a visit by Alexander the Great to Corinth. There, the story goes, the emperor of the known world encountered the famous Cynic philosopher Diogenes looking attentively at a pile of human bones. Alexander asked the philosopher what he was hoping to see in those bones. Diogenes's reply was, "I'm looking for that which I cannot find—the difference between your father's bones and those of his slaves."

At the heart of the philosopher's comment is the

awareness that death comes to everyone. It is no respecter of rank, wealth, or talent. As one clever person put it, "The death rate among humans is still stuck at 100 percent." But there is more than one kind of death.

When God warned Adam and Eve about the tree of the knowledge of good and evil, He said, "For in the day that thou eatest thereof thou shalt surely die" (Genesis 2:17). Yet they didn't drop dead in their tracks when they violated that command. But as we've seen throughout the pages of this book, they died that day in a myriad of ways. On that day physical death became an inevitability for them and for their billions of offspring yet unborn. Paul lays this out clearly in the fifth chapter of Romans:

- "Therefore, just as through one man sin entered the world, and death through sin, and thus death spread to all men, because all sinned..." (Romans 5:12, NKJV).

- "Nevertheless death reigned from Adam to Moses..." (Romans 5:14, NKJV).

- "For if by the one man's offense many died..." (Romans 5:15, NKJV).

- "For if by the one man's offense death reigned through the one..." (Romans 5:17, NKJV).

- "Therefore, as through one man's offense judgment came to all men, resulting in condemnation..." (Romans 5:18, NKJV).

- "For as by one man's disobedience many
  were made sinners..." (Romans 5:19, NKJV).

Death's reign began on planet Earth on the day Adam fell. That rule continued unchallenged and uninterrupted until death forfeited its right to dominion by taking One it had no legal right to take—One who was not infected by the first Adam's disease of sin.

It seems contradictory, but every one of us was born both dying and already dead—dying in the sense that, as we've already observed, the death rate among humans remains stubbornly at 100 percent. "It is appointed unto men once to die, but after this the judgment" (Hebrews 9:27).

Yet in another very real and very important sense, every person walking the crusty surface of this people planet today is *already* dead—unless we've come to the cross and made the great exchange of His life for our death. We stand with the Ephesians, of whom Paul said, "You were dead in your trespasses and sins." Isn't it fitting and ironic that a culture in which zombie and vampire movies are wildly popular would be filled with people who are themselves a type of "walking dead"?

Finally, those who have not experienced the second birth will face an eternal death at the end of this brief wisp of time and activity we call life. It is a tragedy of unspeakable proportions. It is a tragedy God sent Jesus to prevent. It is the cause of the cross. At that tree Jesus made it possible for us to exchange our deaths in every form. We can trade our life of walking death for one in which we're fully alive in every way. "The thief cometh not, but for to steal, and to kill, and to destroy," Jesus announced. "I am come that they might have life, and that they might have it more abundantly [sufficient in quantity, superior in quality]" (John 10:10).

Not only does the blood of Calvary's crucified Lamb make us spiritually alive, but also in His victory over Satan He removes the sting of physical death. As the writer of Hebrews explains:

> Inasmuch then as the children have partaken of flesh and blood, He Himself likewise shared in the same, that through death He might destroy him who had the power of death, that is, the devil, and release those who through fear of death were all their lifetime subject to bondage.
>
> —HEBREWS 2:14–15, NKJV

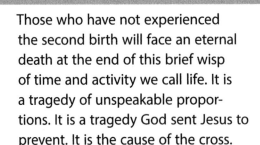

Those who have not experienced the second birth will face an eternal death at the end of this brief wisp of time and activity we call life. It is a tragedy of unspeakable proportions. It is a tragedy God sent Jesus to prevent. It is the cause of the cross.

For the saints who make the great exchange at Calvary, death loses all its power to terrify. Thus countless Christian martyrs have faced the threat of death from tyrants and demon-spawned political systems with grace and courage. Something profound and inexplicable happens in the soul of a believer when he or she fully grasps the truth of this beautiful Bible promise:

Behold, I tell you a mystery: We shall not all sleep, but we shall all be changed—in a moment, in the twinkling of an eye, at the last trumpet. For the trumpet will sound, and the dead will be raised incorruptible, and we shall be changed. For this corruptible must put on incorruption, and this mortal must put on immortality. So when this corruptible has put on incorruption, and this mortal must put on immortality, then shall be brought to pass the saying that is written: "Death is swallowed up in victory."

"O Death, where is your sting?
O Hades, where is your victory?"
—1 Corinthians 15:51–55, nkjv

F. B. Meyer, a fiery Baptist preacher born in England in the mid-1800s, had just been informed by his doctor that he had an untreatable condition and that death was imminent. With sublime peace and serenity, he pulled out his stationery and wrote the following note to one of his dearest old friends and colleagues in ministry. His words reveal the supreme confidence in the face of death itself that is the birthright of every person who has knelt to accept this, the greatest of exchanges, at Calvary's cross:

I have just heard, to my great surprise, that I have but a few days to live. It may be that before this reaches you, I shall have entered the palace. Don't trouble to write. We shall meet in the morning.[7]

THE SCANDAL OF THE CROSS

Chapter 6

Then came the cross. It leveled all distinctions;
it burst through all barriers of nationality.
There was neither Jew nor Gentile, Greek nor
barbarian, but Christ was all and in all.... One
feels in an instant the insult of it all.[1]
—GEORGE H. MORRISON
(1866–1928)

THE CROSS IS offensive. Its implications, an outrage. Its message, scandalous.

These are not the assertions of a postmodern skeptic or a humanistic university professor. This is the plain declaration of the Bible.

To first-century ears the proclamation that God Himself had come in human form and then been killed in an unspeakably shameful way was usually met with either sputtering, offended disbelief, or dismissive ridicule. Thus Paul told the believers in cosmopolitan Corinth, "But we preach Christ crucified, to Jews a stumbling block and to Gentiles foolishness" (1 Corinthians 1:23, NAS).

The Greek word translated "stumbling block" in Paul's statement is *skandalon*. It is obviously the root of our

English word *scandal*, but it actually describes a thing that causes a person to trip or is an obstacle that stands in his path. Anyone who has brutally "stubbed" a toe walking across a dark room in the middle of the night has encountered a literal *skandalon*. So has any hiker who has rounded a curve on a narrow mountain trail only to find a recently fallen boulder blocking the path.

The message of Jesus and the cross was a stone of stumbling for the religious, tradition-loving Jews and an absurdity to the trendy, intellectual Greeks. Those are essentially the same two responses of all who reject that message today.

As we saw in the opening chapter, many religious-minded people—including many who readily accept Jesus as a teacher and Jesus as a champion of the poor and oppressed—reject the clear message of the cross. Liberal theologian and pastor Robin Meyers encapsulates this view in his book *Saving Jesus From the Church*. In a chapter titled "The Cross as Futility, Not Forgiveness," he writes:

> Forget for a moment that we no longer believe in the idea of blood atonement. Think what this view says about God. First, God must not be both all-powerful and all-loving, or God would not require such a sacrifice in order to be restored to his own creation. Second, if this "had to happen," then we are dealing with a deity who not only must play by our rules but is, at best, capable of being bribed or, at worst, guilty of divine child abuse.[2]

Yes, after two millennia the cross is still causing religious elites to stumble. Its clear message remains an obstacle some modern thinkers simply can't "get over," so they try mightily to get around it.

To others—like the Greeks of old—the cross is foolishness. Today's new breed of self-styled skeptics and militant atheists see nothing in the cross but fodder for clever mockeries and deliberately shocking blasphemies. The patron saint of these may be the late comic George Carlin, who once famously said, "I would never want to be a member of a group whose symbol was a guy nailed to two pieces of wood." But an unending stream of imitators battle to top each other in portraying the most loving and selfless act ever rendered to undeserving humanity as something ridiculous.

> After two millennia the cross is still causing religious elites to stumble. Its clear message remains an obstacle some modern thinkers simply can't "get over," so they try mightily to get around it.

Many observant Jews of Paul's day, and of ours, reject the cross and its implications. As do Muslims. To many first-century Jews it was impossible to reconcile their concept of the Messiah with an accursed death on "a tree." And many modern Jews view the message of the cross through the lens of historical persecutions at the hands of the medieval Roman Catholic church. Meanwhile, Muslims profess to honor Jesus as a prophet but stumble on the cross as well. Indeed, Islam explicitly rejects the assertion that Jesus died on a cross. (Nevertheless both Jews and Muslims around the world are coming to Christ by the thousands each day.)

The fact is, people of all stripes and backgrounds view the cross as either stumbling block or foolishness. But why? What is it about the message of the cross that is so scandalous? So unacceptable? So offensive? Here are a few of the reasons.

The cross is an affront to man's pride.

There is something deeply ingrained in fallen man's arrogant, self-aggrandizing heart that demands a better, nobler, prettier narrative than the cross offers.

The religious leaders of Judah in Jesus's day had their hearts set on a superhero deliverer. They looked for a new King David or Judas "The Hammer" Maccabeus who would awaken the dormant warriors of Israel and shatter their Roman shackles. It was a Messiah-concept befitting their self-image. Similarly, in our culture of super-hero worship, our modern egos demand a savior that conquers in might and grandeur, not One who humbles Himself in foot-washing servanthood and willing surrender to the occupiers.

The nineteenth-century Scottish preacher George Morrison recognized this tension and described it this way:

> If I know anything about the ideals men cherish now, and about the hopes that reign in ten thousand hearts, they are as antagonistic to the cross as was the Jewish ideal of Messiah. Written across Calvary is *sacrifice*; written across this age of ours

is *pleasure.* On the lips of Christ are the stern words, *I must die.* On the lips of this age of ours, *I must enjoy.*[3]

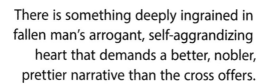

There is something deeply ingrained in fallen man's arrogant, self-aggrandizing heart that demands a better, nobler, prettier narrative than the cross offers.

Jesus said if you want to lead, be the servant of all. Jesus humbled Himself in coming. Paul reminds us in Philippians 2:7–8 that Jesus "took upon him the form of a servant, and was made in the likeness of men: And being found in fashion as a man, he humbled himself, and became obedient unto death, even the death of the cross."

We find no chest thumping or high-fiving at the cross. There are no end-zone dances or self-congratulatory speeches. Many today find the cross offensive because it cuts against the prideful spirit of the age.

The cross is an affront to man's fallen wisdom and intellect.

As Paul declared to the believers at Corinth, "For the preaching of the cross is to them that perish foolishness" (1 Corinthians 1:18). If the message of Calvary seemed ridiculous to the Greeks of Paul's day, how much more do today's intellectuals, sophisticates, and deep thinkers view it as an absurdity. Paul continues:

> For it is written, I will destroy the wisdom of the
> wise, and will bring to nothing the understanding
> of the prudent. Where is the wise? Where is the
> scribe? Where is the disputer of this world? Hath
> not God made foolish the wisdom of this world?
> —1 CORINTHIANS 1:19–20

Oh, how fallen men love to build elaborate philosophical conjectures and complex ontological and epistemological constructs—all meticulously crafted to avoid acknowledging that man is fallen and can't get up in his own strength. Oh, how the modern mind loves an Oprahized brand of "spirituality" designed to help us all feel good about ourselves. Our universities and seminaries are filled with smart, credentialed people who have "grown" beyond taking the Bible's claims about man and sin and the Savior seriously.

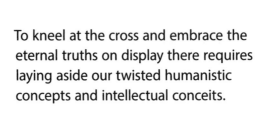

To kneel at the cross and embrace the
eternal truths on display there requires
laying aside our twisted humanistic
concepts and intellectual conceits.

The problem is that human wisdom has become corrupted and is built upon a deeply flawed foundation. As Paul established at that outset of his sweeping treatise on Christian doctrine—his letter to the believers in Rome, the smartest of the very brightest of humanity: "...became vain in their imaginations, and their foolish heart was darkened. Professing themselves to be wise, they became fools" (Romans 1:21–22).

To kneel at the cross and embrace the eternal truths on display there requires laying aside our twisted humanistic concepts and intellectual conceits. There we embrace mystery. There we behold a simple story that unfolds in a universe founded upon holy laws by a holy God.

A crime. A penalty paid by an innocent substitute. A free offer of restoration and renewal. A story so simple a little child can comprehend it. Too simple, in fact, for many of the intellects of this upside-down age.

The cross is also an affront to man's religious self-righteousness.

The cross is a stumbling block for many because it offends man's *religious* pride. Ever since the first sinners sewed fig leaves together in an effort to cover their shame, fallen people have been working and striving and creating in a vain effort to do for themselves what only a Redeemer could do. From the tower of Babel, intended to carry man back to heaven with a monument to his own ingenuity to the golden calf forged by the Israelites during the Exodus, to Islam's five-pillared system of works, to Catholicism's system of penances and rosaries, to modern socialism's futile efforts to build a utopian society through government control and central planning—the root of the impulse is ever and always the same. A pride- and shame-fueled need to get back to the garden through our own efforts. To earn it. To deserve it. To be able to look down on our struggling neighbor and say, "I'm doing better than you."

The Pharisees in Jesus's day took great satisfaction in what they believed was their obsessive meeting of all God's requirements for righteousness. They observed all the festivals and holidays. They met the dietary requirements and followed the ritual washing protocols. They tithed so meticulously—right down to the mint and cumin in the spice cabinet. They kept the Sabbath fanatically, avoiding all "work" as defined in the broadest possible way. Yet Jesus took one look at these and said, "Woe to you, scribes and Pharisees, hypocrites! For you are like whitewashed tombs which on the outside appear beautiful, but inside they are full of dead men's bones and all uncleanness" (Matthew 23:27, NAS).

The message of the cross is that we were and are and always will be helpless to effect our own salvation. But that is a message man's religious pride cannot abide.

The religious mind stumbles at the simple demand made by the cross—i.e., stop trying in your own strength. Just come and receive. Jesus said, "Come unto me, all ye that labour and are heavy laden, and I will give you rest. Take my yoke upon you, and learn of me; for I am meek and lowly in heart: and ye shall find rest unto your souls.

For my yoke is easy, and my burden is light" (Matthew 11:28–30).

The message of the cross is that we were and are and always will be helpless to effect our own salvation. But that is a message man's religious pride cannot abide.

In the mid-1700s the great open-air revivalist George Whitefield was preaching in a field outside of Boston. In attendance was a well-to-do lady of breeding and high standing in the community—although she was not a Christian. She had heard about Bostonians flocking in the thousands to listen to this English preaching phenomenon, so she came out to hear for herself. Whitefield preached of Christ's sacrifice for sinners and how "all we like sheep have gone astray." He closed his message with the words he always used. An invitation: "Come, poor, lost, undone sinner, come just as you are to Christ."

The woman was furious and stormed back to her waiting carriage in a rage: "It is perfectly intolerable that ladies like me should be spoken to just like some creature from the streets!"

The message of the cross *is* intolerable to those who prefer to think they can obtain real righteousness through their own efforts. It *is* offensive. It is a love so deep and free that it is scandalous.

In his book *The Furious Longing of God* Brennan Manning, a former Catholic priest, tells of an extraordinary event he witnessed while ministering at North America's only leper colony in Carville, Louisiana. From his home in New Orleans he would visit the colony regularly, going from room to room to visit and pray with the patients there.

On one cloudy, rain-soaked day Manning's arrival at the colony was met by a frantic nurse. "Come quickly!" she blurted. "Can you come pray for Yolanda? She's dying, Brennan. She's dying." Pulling out a vial of anointing oil he carried with him at all times, Manning hurried up the stairs to the room of a Hispanic woman he had spoken with on numerous occasions.

Yolanda was thirty-seven. Leprosy (or Hansen's disease, as it is officially called today) had begun its insidious work upon her face and body five years earlier. Manning had seen photographs of her from that earlier time. In Manning's words:

> ...she must have been one of the most stunningly beautiful creatures God ever made. I do not mean just a cute, pretty, or even attractive woman. I mean the kind of blinding physical beauty that causes men and women on the street to stop and stare. In pictures, Yolanda had the largest, most mesmerizing, most translucent brown eyes I've ever seen, set in this exquisitely chiseled face with high cheekbones.... But that was then.[4]

The woman Manning saw on that day had very little of her nose remaining, and her lipless mouth was twisted into a permanent grimace. Her once waist-length hair was mostly absent save a few wispy clumps. Her ears were misshapen lumps. Her arms terminated in two stumps where graceful hands and fingers had once been.

Manning entered the room and found the dying woman alone. She'd had a husband once, but he'd divorced her two years earlier in horror and revulsion at what the disease had made her. They'd had two sons together—now fourteen and sixteen—but their father had forbidden them to ever see her again. And they had not.

She was dying. Alone. Abandoned.

Manning anointed Yolanda with oil and prayed for her. Then, as he turned away to replace the oil bottle's cap, the room was suddenly filled with bright light. His first thought was that the sun had finally broken through and was now streaming through the window, but a glance in that direction revealed that clouds still hung thick and gray. Then he turned and looked at Yolanda.

> ...if I live to be three hundred years old I'll never be able to find the words to describe what I saw—her face was like a sunburst over the mountains, like one thousand sunbeams streaming out of her face literally so brilliant I had to shield my eyes.[5]

Manning looked at her a moment and said, "Yolanda, you appear to be very happy."

"Oh, Father, I am SO happy," she replied in her Mexican-accented English. He asked her why, and she explained: "The Abba of Jesus just told me that He would take me home today." For a few moments Manning couldn't speak. Tears of wonder and joy and gratitude flowed down his face as he witnessed the luminescent ecstasy and glory that only a word from the Father can produce in one of His children. Eventually he was able to ask, "What did the Abba of Jesus say to you?" Her response stunned him:

He said,

"Come now, my love. My lovely one. Come.
For the winter has passed,
The snows are over and gone,
the flowers appear in the land,
the season of joyful songs has come.
The cooing of the turtledove is heard in our land.
Come now, my love. My Yolanda, come.
Let me see your face. And let me hear your voice,
for your voice is sweet and your face is beautiful.
Come now, my love,
my lovely one,
Come."

Six hours later Yolanda's little leprous body was swept into the furious love of her Abba.[6]

Manning recognized the words. They were from the Song of Solomon, chapter 2. It was a very close paraphrase of verses 10 through 14, though not exactly like any translation he knew. It is a passage that depicts a man in love coming to take away a beautiful, adored woman so they can be together forever.

Later that day Manning would learn that Yolanda was illiterate. She had never read a book in her life, and certainly not a Bible. No one, to anyone's knowledge, had ever read the Bible to her.

In other words, in her final moments, this poor, disfigured, abandoned woman received a visit by a loving Father God and heard words of love and kindness directly from His holy lips: "Come, My lovely one. Let Me see your face."

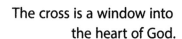

The cross is a window into the heart of God.

Oh, what a scandalous love is this…this relentless love of a God for a rebellious race. For in a sense we are all Yolanda. Every son and daughter of Adam has been ravaged by the disfiguring, debilitating leprosy of sin. We're all abandoned, unloved, lonely, and dying—whether we recognize it or not. Yet through Calvary's cross Abba steps into our ugliness and desolation whispering, "Come be with Me. Let's walk together in My garden in the cool of the day."

As the saints of a forgotten generation used to sing:

> O love of God, how rich, how pure!
> How measureless and strong.
> It shall forevermore endure
> The saints' and the angels' song.
>
> Could we with ink the ocean fill,
> And were the skies of parchment made,
> Were every stalk on earth a quill,
> And every man a scribe by trade,
> To write the love of God above,
> Would drain the ocean dry. Nor could the scroll
>   contain the whole,
> Though stretched from sky to sky.

O love of God, how rich, how pure!
How measureless and strong.
It shall forevermore endure
The saints' and the angels' song.[7]

The cross is a window into the heart of God. Some look and are offended. Some look and cry, "Foolishness!" But some see love on display. These come and lay their burdens down. These come and live.

TAKING UP
THE CROSS

Chapter 7

The Lord help you to bow your spirit in submission to the divine will ere you fall asleep this night, so that waking with to-morrow's sun, you may go forth to the day's cross with the holy and submissive spirit which becomes a follower of the Crucified.[1]

—CHARLES SPURGEON
(1831–1892)

O N OUR JOURNEY to this point we have seen that a gospel that does not have the cross at its center is really no gospel at all. We have observed with sadness the tendency of modern Christians to shove both the symbol and the message of the cross to the periphery of our faith. And how some would even twist and distort that wondrous message to make it more palatable to a seductive, let's-all-feel-good-about-ourselves culture.

We have seen that Calvary is the axis of human history—the culmination of God's millennia-long grand strategy to wrest back control of earth and man from the enemy con man who had obtained legal rights through subterfuge. We have dared to take a hard, sobering look at the process of crucifixion to understand what Jesus suffered in natural terms. Then we pulled back the curtain of the spirit world to glimpse what was taking place at Calvary in the realm of angels and demons.

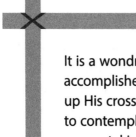

It is a wondrous thing to survey all Jesus accomplished for us when He took up His cross, but it is equally sobering to contemplate that following Jesus means taking up a cross of our own.

We have stood silent and awestruck at the nail-pierced feet of the suffering Savior and listened to His final statements. As the wounded Word Incarnate pays an awful price just to speak, we've treasured and examined and embraced each truth-rich phrase. With swelling gratitude and wonder we have done an accounting of all Jesus accomplished for us on the cross. We have taken a holy inventory of the embarrassment of riches on offer in exchange for our abject poverty.

Yes, it is a wondrous thing to survey all Jesus accomplished for us when He took up His cross. But it is equally sobering to contemplate that following Jesus means taking up a cross of our own. But it's true.

"Take up your cross..."

On several occasions in the course of His ministry Jesus used this language with His disciples. In each instance

Jesus linked the act of taking up the cross to the act of *following* Him.

In the tenth chapter of Matthew we find Jesus giving the Twelve some last-minute instruction before sending them out on their own to minister for the first time. He imparts some of His power to them (Matthew 10:1). He provides them with both their message and their method: "And as you go, preach, saying, 'The kingdom of heaven is at hand.' Heal the sick, cleanse the lepers, raise the dead, cast out demons. Freely you have received, freely give" (Matthew 10:7–8, NKJV). He warns them about the hostility and opposition they will face—"sheep in the midst of wolves" He calls them (Matthew 10:16).

Then He gives them a glimpse of the intense persecution they will one day face: "...for they will deliver you up to councils and scourge you in their synagogues. You will be brought before governors and kings.... And you will be hated by all for My name's sake" (Matthew 10:17–18, 22, NKJV). The Master continues in what is surely the most depressing pregame pep talk any team of men has ever received from their coach. He goes on to instruct them that when they are persecuted in one city, they must flee to the next one. The wide-eyed disciples hear Jesus tell them that He did not come to bring peace to the earth but rather a sword (Matthew 10:34). He paints a distressing picture of households being torn in half because some members love Him and others hate Him (Matthew 10:35–36).

Finally, if all that weren't sobering enough, Jesus verbally draws a line in the sand and warns that crossing that line—choosing Him—means forsaking everything else:

> He who loves father or mother more than Me is not
> worthy of Me. And he who loves son or daughter
> more than Me is not worthy of Me. And *he who
> does not take his cross and follow after Me* is not
> worthy of Me. He who finds his life will lose it, and
> he who loses his life for My sake will find it.
>
> —MATTHEW 10:37–39, NKJV,
> EMPHASIS ADDED

You have to wonder what the disciples made of Jesus's
use of the phrase "take His cross." Did they already know
how Jesus was going to die? How many crucified men had
they passed as they walked the roads between Galilee and
Judea? How many times had they witnessed a convicted
criminal or rebel being forced by Roman soldiers to carry
a crossbeam through the street?

We don't know what meaning the disciples attached
to that phrase. But we know that Jesus used it with them
again a few months later—this time as Jesus's own crucifixion is approaching.

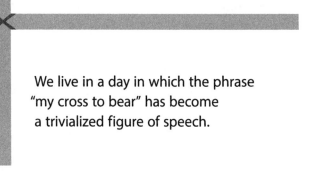

We live in a day in which the phrase
"my cross to bear" has become
a trivialized figure of speech.

In Matthew chapter 16, Simon Peter has just received
the revelation that Jesus is indeed the promised Messiah
of God (Matthew 16:16–17). Then Jesus states plainly and

in detail that He is about to go to Jerusalem where He will suffer, be killed, and be raised on the third day (Matthew 16:21). Peter objects to that plan and tries to throw himself in front of it. Jesus rebukes him, turns to the disciples, and makes this proclamation:

> If anyone desires to come after Me, let him deny himself, and take up his cross, and follow Me. For whoever desires to save his life will lose it, but whoever loses his life for My sake will find it. For what profit is it to a man if he gains the whole world, and loses his own soul? Or what will a man give in exchange for his soul?
>
> —MATTHEW 16:24–26, NKJV

Luke's account of this same statement adds one additional word: "…let him deny himself, and take up his cross *daily*…" (Luke 9:23, NKJV, emphasis added).

We live in a day in which the phrase "my cross to bear" has become a trivialized figure of speech. People who have never crossed the threshold of a church or cracked open a Bible use the phrase to describe anything that is an ongoing annoyance in their lives. Foot bunions, lazy husbands, cranky bosses, dry skin, and loud children have all been proclaimed to be crosses that must be borne. In the modern vernacular, the concept of carrying one's cross has been twisted and abused into a mere affliction—in much the same way Paul's "thorn in the flesh" and Solomon's "fly in the ointment" have been misappropriated, abused, and robbed of meaning.

Still, Jesus's words meant something quite profound and serious when He said them. And they are recorded in our Gospels for a reason. They have meaning for those of us who hear a call to "follow Jesus" today. But what is it? What does it mean to "take up our crosses" for those of us who refuse to be swept along in the cultural current of a cross-less generation of "Christians"?

Surely Jesus did not mean that we are to literally carry around heavy beams of wood as we go about our daily routines. There is certainly no evidence that His disciples ever did that. Does it mean that we are to become like the extreme Roman Catholic "flagellants" in the Philippine province of Pampanga who during the season of Lent each year beat themselves on the back with rods and whips until bloody, and even drive small nails through their own hands, all in hopes of earning an additional measure of forgiveness from God by identifying with Jesus in His suffering?

> Cross carrying involves self-denial—
> choosing to say no to our own desires
> and pursue God's desires instead.
> It means choosing to lay aside our
> personal agendas and embracing
> God's grand agenda of the ages.

Of course not. Any interpretation of cross-carrying that would try to add to the extraordinary redemptive work that Jesus accomplished for us on the cross is an insult to Him and an affront to the gospel. When Jesus said, "It is finished," He meant what He said.

Nevertheless, I believe there are three key implications

in Jesus's exhortation for us to take up the cross. And having an understanding of these implications will equip us to live lives of maximum impact, purpose, and meaning.

The first key to Jesus's meaning is made evident in the words we heard Him use in Matthew 16, above. This was the second time Jesus had sternly stated that anyone who intended to follow Him needed to be prepared to "take up His cross." But that time He preceded that phrase with some words that offer us tremendous insight into what He meant.

He said that anyone who intended to be a Jesus follower must be prepared to *"deny himself,* and take up his cross." The clear implication here is that cross carrying involves self-denial—choosing to say no to our own desires and pursue God's desires instead. It means choosing to lay aside our personal agendas and embracing God's grand agenda of the ages.

In other words, it means not letting our personal appetites, egos, and itches rule our choices. But could anything be more anathema to the spirit of this age? Here in America we've taken a culture built upon the blood and sweat of pioneers and gradually transformed it into the land of the self-indulgent, self-absorbed, and self-aggrandizing. It is a consumer culture built upon an overarching advertising message that says, "Buy this for yourself. You deserve it. (Charge it if necessary.)"

In the third chapter of Philippians, Paul talks about a type of self-styled pseudo-Christian who was already infiltrating the young church. People who were slaves to their appetites. People, "whose end is destruction, whose God is their belly, and whose glory is in their shame, who mind earthly things" (Philippians 3:19).

Paul had a label for people such as these. In the preceding verse he declared, "They are the enemies of the cross of Christ" (Philippians 3:18).

Do you see it? A refusal to deny ourselves makes us enemies of the cross, just as Jesus's words suggest that a willingness to do so makes us a friend of the cross.

Jesus understood well the link between self-denial and a willingness to carry the cross. That is the heart of the battle Jesus would soon wage in the Garden of Gethsemane. There He modeled self-denial when He cried out, "Not my will but thine." As Leonard Ravenhill once stated, "Gethsemane is where He died; the cross is only the evidence."[2]

A refusal to deny ourselves makes us enemies of the cross, just as Jesus's words suggest that a willingness to do so makes us a friend of the cross.

In his classic book *Discipleship*, Dietrich Bonhoeffer wrote: "Self-denial means knowing only Christ, no longer knowing oneself. It means no longer oneself, only him who is going ahead of us, no longer seeing the way which is too difficult for us. Self-denial says only: he is going ahead; hold fast to him."[3]

In saying, "*If* anyone desires to come after Me..." Jesus makes it clear that it is a choice. And by saying, as Luke reports, "...let him take up his cross *daily*...," Jesus lets us know it is a choice we must make anew each morning.

The first implication of carrying the cross is willingness to live a life worthy of His sacrifice by being self-sacrificial.

The second aspect of cross carrying involves a willingness to endure hardship, persecution, and rejection for the name of Christ. As the American Founding Father William Penn, a devout Quaker, once wrote: "No pain, no palm; no thorns, no throne; no gall, no glory; no cross, no crown."[4]

Each time Jesus presented His disciples with the challenge to take up the cross, He embedded that challenge in sobering warnings about future persecution and hardship. He wanted them to know there is a cost to following Him. What Bonhoeffer called "the cost of discipleship" is not a price we pay for our salvation in any way. Salvation and its myriad benefits are the free "gift of God: not of works, lest any man should boast" (Ephesians 2:8–9).

No, we don't merit God's acceptance through suffering. But once we are accepted and made whole through our identification with Jesus, we then become partakers in His rejection precisely because we *are* identified with Him. This is exactly what Jesus told His disciples in the fifteenth chapter of John:

> If the world hate you, ye know that it hated me before it hated you. If ye were of the world, the world would love his own: but because ye are not of the world, but I have chosen you out of the world,

therefore the world hateth you. Remember the word
that I said unto you, The servant is not greater than
his lord. If they have persecuted me, they will also
persecute you; if they have kept my saying, they
will keep yours also. But all these things will they
do unto you for my name's sake, because they know
not him that sent me.

—JOHN 15:18–21

There is unspeakable benefit to being "in Christ" and
Him in us—peace, purpose, provision, joy, hope, and
eternity in heaven too! But there is also a cost—rejection
by the world and those in slavery to the world's system.
Too many believers today want the former without the
latter. They want to enjoy all the perks and blessings of
being a Jesus follower but still be invited to sit at the "cool
kids' table" of this depraved culture. They want to be well
thought of by Hollywood's godless media elites and the
Ivy League's humanist academics and Madison Avenue's
hedonistic style setters.

We cannot have it both ways. James pulled no punches
when he thundered, "Ye adulterers and adulteresses, know
ye not that the friendship of the world is enmity with
God? Whosoever therefore will be a friend of the world is
the enemy of God" (James 4:4).

This is a choice Christians in non-Western countries
know much better than we believers in the United States.
In Iran, Pakistan, Iraq, and throughout the Islamic world,
choosing Christ means an open-eyed choice to risk torture and death. Here, we get the vapors if someone makes
fun of us. Bonhoeffer says:

The cross is not adversity, nor the harshness of fate, but suffering coming solely from our commitment to Jesus Christ. The suffering of the cross is not fortuitous, but necessary. The cross is not the suffering tied to natural existence, but the suffering tied to being Christians. The cross is never simply a matter of suffering, but a matter of suffering and rejection, and even, strictly speaking, rejection for the sake of Jesus Christ...[5]

> There is unspeakable benefit to being "in Christ" and Him in us. But there is also a cost—rejection by the world and those in slavery to the world's system.

The second implication of carrying the cross is willingness to suffer rejection by those who reject the One we love, serve and follow.

✝ ✝ ✝ ✝ ✝

Finally, taking up our crosses means cultivating a love for the things Jesus loves. And more than anything else, He has a heart for the lost and dying of this world. We have already visited His parable of the lost sheep, the lost coin, and the lost son. In His own words, He came "to seek and to save that which was lost" (Luke 19:10).

In a very real sense, taking up our crosses means wanting to see Jesus's extraordinary sacrifice bear maximum fruit in the cause for which He suffered and died. It means an intense desire to see not a single drop of Jesus's precious blood wasted because someone failed to have an opportunity to hear and receive the redemption He purchased for him or her at Calvary. This is a conviction the Moravian Christians of Europe knew well. They called it bringing Jesus "the reward of His suffering."

The Moravian Christians were a persecuted Christian movement in Central Europe that emerged well before the Protestant Reformation. A century before Martin Luther nailed his convictions to the Wittenberg door, the Moravians were quietly recognizing and rejecting the abuses and errors of Rome. In response they pursued a simple faith of worship and charity. As a result, they were severely persecuted, and they suffered great hardship. Indeed, the founder of the movement, John Hus, was tried by a Roman Catholic council and burned alive in 1415.

The Moravians understood what "taking up the cross" meant. And they are marked by history for their extraordinary compassion, service to the poor and oppressed, and above all, their passion for souls.

It was in the early eighteenth century that Moravian believers first came to the New World. Persecution drove some across the Atlantic. But many others were compelled by a Christ-honoring heart for souls. Some saw the waves of African slaves being transported to the Americas and pondered how these most pitiful of souls might be brought the light of the gospel.

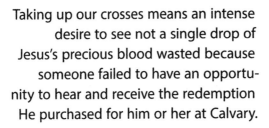

Taking up our crosses means an intense
desire to see not a single drop of
Jesus's precious blood wasted because
someone failed to have an opportunity to hear and receive the redemption
He purchased for him or her at Calvary.

Of course, the treatment of slaves was almost universally appalling. But the colonial plantations of the West
Indies were notorious for their cruelty. Because the supply
of fresh human property from Africa seemed almost endless, there was little incentive for Caribbean plantation
owners to provide humane care for their slaves. Therefore
many literally worked their slaves to death and placed
orders with the slavers for replacements. These were the
people the Moravians longed to reach with the hope of
Christ. But how?

Their breathtakingly bold and innovative answer was
to sell themselves into slavery. And so they did. Thus a
Dutch ship with two Moravian missionaries on board
left Copenhagen harbor on October 8, 1732, bound for
the Danish West Indies. John Dober, a potter, and David
Nitschman, a carpenter, were on their way to sell themselves into slavery in hopes of sharing the good news
of the cross with the slaves of the West Indies. History
records that as the ship slid away from her moorings, the
two looked to their friends and loved ones at the dock
and lifted up a cry that would echo in the hearts of future

generations of Moravian missionaries: "May the Lamb
that was slain receive the reward of His suffering!"[6]

Some church historians calculate that eighty thousand
slaves came to Christ through the efforts of Moravian missionaries. They understood what taking up the cross truly
means. The grasped what so many today do not—that following Christ means extending comfort, not seeking to be
comfortable. It means gladly suffering rejection because
Christ too was rejected. It means valuing Christ's sacrifice so much…being so grateful for what He suffered on
our behalves…that we gladly lay down our own lives to
see hell plundered of, and heaven populated with, as many
treasured souls as possible.

Watchman Nee was the great apostle of China and
founder of China's house church movement in the early
decades of the twentieth century. This amazing man of
God knew a little about what it means to take up the cross
and follow the Master—especially after the Communists,
led by Chairman Mao Tse-tung, seized power in 1949 and
launched the first of what would be countless brutal persecutions of that nation's brave believers.

Following Jesus cost Nee a great deal. He spent the last
twenty years of his life as a prisoner in Mao's "reeducation"
camps. Thankfully he was never successfully reeducated.
One of the last people to see him alive was a fellow prisoner Nee had won to Christ. On the eve of the other man's
release, Nee encouraged him to seek out Nee's brother,
Witness Lee, and deliver a message: "Let him know that I
never gave up my faith."

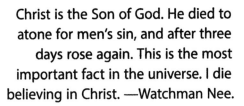

Christ is the Son of God. He died to atone for men's sin, and after three days rose again. This is the most important fact in the universe. I die believing in Christ. —Watchman Nee.

Not long thereafter Watchman Nee was found dead in his prison cell—having succumbed to years of starvation and maltreatment. When the guards removed his body, they found a handwritten note underneath his head. It read:

> Christ is the Son of God. He died to atone for men's sin, and after three days rose again. This is the most important fact in the universe. I die believing in Christ.[7]

So it is. So he did.

Epilogue

Christian, it is your Lord!...he meets the morning
of his resurrection. He arises a conqueror from
the grave; he returns with blessings from the world
of the spirits, he brings salvation to the sons of
men. Never did the returning sun usher in a day
so glorious—it was the jubilee of the universe.[1]
—CHARLES BROOKS
(1813–1883)

CALVARY'S CROSS REPRESENTS the pivotal chapter in God's grand story of loss, love, and redemption. But it is not the final chapter. Let's look with the eyes of the heart and with an imagination informed by and infused with scriptural insight at the events of that extraordinary weekend. Let us play witness to the aftermath of the cross...

Can you see it? They are laying Him in the borrowed tomb of Joseph of Arimathea. "Tear down this temple and I'll build it back in three days," He had prophesied to the uncomprehending Pharisees. Now that temple—His body—has been battered and torn beyond recognition. Loving hands have hurriedly prepared that broken body for burial.

It has been washed and wrapped in strips of linen. The relentlessly sinking sun is setting in the western sky.

So they quickly slide the limp, lifeless, white-shrouded figure onto a chiseled shelf in that rock-hewn tomb. Now as the temple leaders observe, the handpicked guard rolls that massive disk of stone across the opening, and the earth shakes as it drops into place in the niche created to hold it immovable in place.

The co-conspirators seal it, secure it, and tell themselves that they have won...that they have utterly and for all time extinguished the hope of these stubborn Jesus followers. The sun is gone. And the Son is gone. A thick silence envelops the rocky garden, save the distant sound of a woman weeping.

The sun rises and sets once more upon the Judean hills, yet all remains quiet at the sepulcher of the Son of Man. The guards stand vigilant at their posts. Unseen by human eyes, another stands sentry as well. It is death himself keeping watch over the body of the Nazarene. Death dares not delegate this task to an underling. This One is too dangerous. In life the Nazarene had robbed death on more than one occasion. Death will personally see to it that this one does not elude his grasp.

Night falls once more as the rays of a waning full moon glint off the helmets and spear tips of the guards. The enemies of the Christ congratulate themselves on their success at resolving their Galilean problem. Jesus's heartbroken and disillusioned inner circle cowers behind bolted doors. The hosts of heaven look on in breathless suspense—awaiting the next sunrise—and marveling at the mysterious ways of a redemptive God. Quiet and stillness continue to reign in this garden of tombs.

Wait. We hear somebody singing. Oh, it is David, the sweet psalmist of Israel. What is he singing? What is your song, lover of Israel? What is your song?

> Thou wilt not leave my soul in hell,
> nor suffer your darling to see corruption.[2]

Then the morning star, rising in the east, announces the approach of light. The third day begins to dawn on the land. Suddenly the earth trembles to its center, and the powers of heaven are shaken. An angel of God descends, and the guards collapse in terror at his appearing. His countenance is like lightning and his robe is blinding white. Muscular arms roll the stone from the doorway as if it were a child's toy made of paper.

Look! We can see Him now. The Son of God has risen from His bed, but death stands between Him and that open door way. But the Son is moving forward and death is moving backward. Suddenly Jesus leaps toward death. Death attempts to flee out the tomb's doorway, but before he can escape, Jesus reaches toward him and snatches something from death's belted side. The risen One lifts the object heavenward and cries, "Father, these are the keys of death, of hell, and of the grave."

Can you see it? He emerges with a message for you, me, and every fallen, broken, wandering son and daughter of Adam. He declares, "I am Alpha. I am Omega. I am He that liveth, and was dead, and, behold, I am alive forevermore. And because I live, you shall live also!"

That is how our journey to the cross and back ends. Not in defeat but in victory. Not in sorrow but in joy. Not in despair but in abundant hope.

As an old Methodist Episcopal preacher from the Civil War era rightly said:

> The world cannot bury Christ. The earth is not deep enough for His tomb, the clouds are not wide enough for His winding-sheet; He ascends into the heavens, but the heavens cannot contain Him. He still lives—in the church which burns unconsumed with His love; in the truth that reflects His image; in the hearts which burn as He talks with them by the way.[3]

We have been to the cross. Let us walk away changed. Let us take up our crosses and change the world.

Afterword

THIS WAS A book of amen and ouch. Rod Parsley hit the nail on the head and sometimes on the finger. There are people who will rejoice reading it and others who will be upset. But the cross of Christ is the heart of the gospel. All our teaching must relate to that like all the spokes and rim and tires of a wheel relate to the axis. Jesus is the center, the pivot. Everything else will fit into place around Jesus. Indeed, the entire Word of God revolves around Him. If Christ is not the hub, the wheel will wobble and break. People say that we Christians are eccentric. An eccentric object wobbles around a point that is off-center. But that is what the Bible calls "the world." It is not believers, evangelists, witnesses, or Christians who are eccentric, but the world. The world wobbles as it revolves around itself, but the believer is centered on God. When people in the church talk about "making the gospel relevant," they usually mean that we need to show that the gospel has something in common with the world of industry, entertainment, and commerce. They have things back to front. The question is not whether the message can be related to this world, but whether the world is willing to relate to the message of the cross. Relevance is a matter of position and focus. This is another great book from my friend Rod Parsley. I highly recommend it.

—EVANGELIST REINHARD BONNKE, DD
PRESIDENT, CHRIST FOR THE NATIONS

Notes

CHAPTER 1
A CROSS-LESS GENERATION

1. As quoted in *Forty Thousand Quotations, Prose and Poetical*, compiled by Charles Noel Douglas (London: George G. Harrap and Company, Ltd., 1917), 857. Viewed at Google Books.

2. John R. W. Stott, *The Cross of Christ* (Downers Grove, IL: InterVarsity Press, 2006), 71.

3. This quote can be found in numerous books and websites online.

4. Harry E. Fosdick, *Dear Mr. Brown: Letters to a Perplexed Person About Religion* (New York: Harper and Row, 1961), 136.

5. Ibid.

6. Barbara Bradley Hagerty, "Jesus, Reconsidered: Book Sparks Evangelical Debate," NPR.com, March 26, 2010, http://www.npr.org/templates/story/story.php?storyId=125165061 (accessed July 17, 2013).

7. Leif Hansen, "Brian McLaren Interview, Part 1," *The Bleeding Purple* (podcast), January 8, 2006, http://bleedingpurplepodcast.blogspot.com/2006/01/brian-mclaren-interview-part-i.html (accessed July 17, 2013).

8. Alan Jones, *Reimagining Christianity* (Hoboken, NJ: Wiley and Sons, 2005), 132.

9. M. K. Gandhi, *An Autobiography: The Story of My Experiments With Truth* (London: Laurier Books, Ltd., 1927), 113.

10. Charles H. Spurgeon, "The Offence of the Cross," *Spurgeon's Sermons*, vol. 44 (1898).

11. As related in John R. W. Stott, *The Cross of Christ*, 20th anniversary edition (Downers Grove, IL: InterVarsity Press, 1986, 2006), 15. Viewed at Google Books.

12. D. Martyn Lloyd-Jones, *The Cross: God's Way of Salvation* (Wheaton, IL: Crossway Books, 1986), 25–26.

13. J. C. Ryle, *The Cross* (Stirling, Scotland: Drummond's Tract Depot, 1886).

14. FoxNews.com, "Atheist Group Demands Rhode Island City Remove Cross From Atop War Memorial," April 25, 2012, http://www.foxnews.com/us/2012/04/25/atheist-group-wants-cross-from-rhode-island-war-memorial-removed/ (accessed July 17, 2013).

CHAPTER 2
AT THE INTERSECTION OF HEAVEN AND EARTH

1. As quoted in *Forty Thousand Quotations, Prose and Poetical*, 407.

2. James R. Coffey, "The Busiest Intersection in the World: Tokyo's Hachiko Square," January 5, 2011, http://travel.wikinut.com/The-Busiest-Intersection-in-the-World%3A-Tokyo%E2%80%99s-Hachiko-Square/1plo-tr2/ (accessed July 17, 2013).

3. George Campbell Morgan, *The Crises of the Christ* (N.p.: Fleming H. Revell, 1936), 292.

4. Richard John Neuhaus, *Death on a Friday Afternoon* (New York: Basic Books, 2001), 8.

5. Charles H. Spurgeon, "The Death of Christ for His People," in Warren Wiersbe, ed., *Classic Sermons on the Cross of Christ* (Grand Rapids, MI: Hendrickson Publishers, 1990), 57.

6. YouTube.com, "Brennan Manning on God's Love," uploaded by camister69, October 14, 2011, http://www.youtube.com/watch?v=0dMwu1rhTCQ (accessed July 18, 2013).

7. William E. Sangster, "He Dies. He Must Die," in Wiersbe, ed., *Classic Sermons on the Cross of Christ*, 27.

CHAPTER 3
WHY A CROSS?

1. As quoted in Calvin Miller, *Once Upon a Tree* (West Monroe, LA: Howard Publishing, 2002), 151. Viewed at Google Books.

2. Vassilios Tzaferis, "The Archeological Evidence for Crucifixion," in Hershel Shanks, ed., *Jesus: The Last Day* (N.p.: Biblical Archeological Society, 2003), 91–107; as viewed at

Center for Online Judaic Studies, "Crucifixion Bone Fragment, 21 CE," http://www.cojs.org/cojswiki/Crucifixion_Bone_Fragment%2C_21_CE (accessed July 18, 2013).

3. As related by Appian, *Civil Wars* 1.14.121, in Richard Sheppard, "Spartacus Leads Slave Rebellion," OldNewsPublishing.com, http://www.oldnewspublishing.com/spartacus.htm (accessed July 18, 2013).

4. Flavius Josephus, *The Wars of the Jews* 2.5.2, Christian Classics Ethereal Library, http://www.ccel.org/ccel/josephus/complete.iii.iii.v.html (accessed July 18, 2013).

5. Flavius Josephus, *Josephus, the Essential Works: A Condensation of Jewish Antiquities and The Jewish War*, trans. Paul L. Maier (Grand Rapids, MI: Kregel Books, 1994), 358. Viewed at Google Books.

6. "When I Survey the Wondrous Cross" by Isaac Watts. Public domain.

7. See 2 Corinthians 5:21.

8. See Matthew 16:22–23.

9. Neuhaus, *Death on a Friday Afternoon*, 8.

10. See Genesis 3:17–18.

CHAPTER 4
LISTENING AT THE CROSS

1. Robert H. Ireland, *Light From Calvary in the Seven Last Words* (London: James Nisbet and Company, 1873). Viewed at Google Books.

2. As quoted in Greg Laurie, "Famous Last Words—From Voltaire to Christ," World Net Daily Commentary, December 1, 2007, http://www.wnd.com/2007/12/44827/ (accessed July 18, 2013).

3. Justin Wintle and Richard Kenin, eds., *The Dictionary of Biographical Quotation of British and American Subjects* (London: Routledge and Kegan Paul, Ltd., 1978), 12; "The Rock of Ages," *Frank Leslie's Sunday Magazine*, vols. 3–4 (N.p.: Frank Leslie's Publishing House, 1878), 26. Viewed at Google Books.

4. As quoted in Paul Chappell, "Your Last Words," February 4, 2009, http://www.dailyintheword.org/content/your-last-words (accessed July 18, 2013).

5. Ibid.

6. See Luke 2:35.

7. G. Campbell Morgan, "The Darkness of Golgotha," in Wiersbe, ed., *Classic Sermons on the Cross of Christ*, 145.

8. Bible.org, "What Does the Greek Word *Tetelestai* Mean?", https://bible.org/question/what-does-greek-word-tetelestai-mean (accessed July 24, 2013).

9. Charles Spurgeon, "It Is Finished!", sermon 421, delivered December 1, 1861, http://www.spurgeongems.org/vols7-9/chs421 .pdf (accessed July 24, 2013).

10. Romans 8:11.

11. Psalm 16:10.

12. Acts 2:22–24, NKJV.

CHAPTER 5
THE EXCHANGE AT THE CROSS

1. As quoted in Malcolm Duncan, *Risk Takers: The Life God Intends for You* (Oxford, England: Monarch Books, 2012), 130. Viewed at Google Books.

2. "Document: The Purchase of Manhattan Island, 1626," Thirteen.org, http://www.thirteen.org/dutchny/interactives/ manhattan-island/ (accessed July 24, 2013); "Peter Minuit [1580– 1638]," NewNetherlandInstitute.org, http://www .newnetherlandinstitute.org/history-and-heritage/dutch_ americans/peter-minuit/ (accessed July 24, 2013).

3. Adam Pinsker, "Historian Reflects on Alaska Purchase," KTUU.com, June 28, 2013, http://articles.ktuu.com/2013-06-28/ anchorage-museum_40261287 (accessed July 24, 2013); "Treaty With Russia for the Purchase of Alaska," Primary Documents in American History, Library of Congress, http://www.loc.gov/rr/ program/bib/ourdocs/Alaska.html (accessed July 24, 2013).

4. MLB.com, "World Series History: Championships by Club," http://mlb.mlb.com/mlb/history/postseason/mlb_ws.jsp?feature=club_champs (accessed July 24, 2013); MLB.com, "World Series History: AL Club Summaries," http://mlb.mlb.com/mlb/history/postseason/mlb_ws.jsp?feature=al_clubs (accessed July 24, 2013).

5. Blaise Pascal, *Pascal's Pensées* (Hamburg, Germany: Tredition Classics, 2012), section 7, "Morality and Doctrine." Viewed at Google Books.

6. See Psalm 118:22; Matthew 21:42; Acts 4:11.

7. As quoted in Mrs. Charles B. Cowan, *Consolation* (N.p.: Oriental Missionary Society, 1932), 70.

CHAPTER 6
THE SCANDAL OF THE CROSS

1. George H. Morrison, "The Offense of the Cross," http://articles.ochristian.com/article525.shtml (accessed July 24, 2013).

2. Robin Meyers, *Saving Jesus From the Church* (New York: HarperCollins, 2009), 69.

3. George H. Morrison, "The Offense of the Cross," in Wiersbe, ed., *Classic Sermons on the Cross of Christ*, 50–51.

4. Brennan Manning, *The Furious Longing of God* (Colorado Springs, CO: David C. Cook, 2009), 54.

5. Ibid., 55.

6. Ibid., 56.

7. "The Love of God" by Frederick M. Lehman. Public domain.

CHAPTER 7
TAKING UP THE CROSS

1. Charles H. Spurgeon, *Works of Charles Haddon (C. H.) Spurgeon*, "February 25, PM," Google ebook. Viewed at Google Books.

2. Leonard Ravenhill, "Are We Willing to Drink His Cup?," sermon preached 1985, quoted as maxim at Ravenhill.org,

"Maxims #7," http://www.ravenhill.org/maxims7.htm (accessed July 25, 2013).

3. Dietrich Bonhoeffer, *Discipleship* (Minneapolis, MN: Fortress Press, 2003), 80. Viewed at Google Books.

4. William Penn, *No Cross, No Crown*, as quoted in Barbara A. Somervill, *William Penn: Founder of Pennsylvania* (N.p.: Capstone, 2006), 37. Viewed at Google Books.

5. Dietrich Bonhoeffer, *Meditations on the Cross* (Louisville, KY: Westminster John Knox Press, 1998), 13. Viewed at Google Books.

6. Claude Hickman, "Count Zinzendorf," HistoryMakers.info, http://www.historymakers.info/inspirational-christians/count-zinzendorf.html (accessed July 25, 2013).

7. Ron Durham, *Ancient Words: A Biblical Synoptic and Commentary* (N.p.: Xulon Press, 2011), 151.

EPILOGUE

1. Charles Brooks, *Daily Monitor, or, Reflections for Each Day in the Year* (Boston: N. S. Simpkins, and Co., 1828), 310. Viewed at Google Books.

2. See Psalm 16:10.

3. Edward Thomson, "Christ: Resurrection and Exaltation," in Josiah H. Gilbert, ed., *Dictionary of Burning Words of Brilliant Writers* (New York: Wilbur B. Ketcham, 1895), 76.